Seeking to Make the World Anew

Poems of the Living Dialectic

Sam Friedman

Hamilton Books
A member of
The Rowman & Littlefield Publishing Group
Lanham · Boulder · New York · Toronto · Plymouth, UK

Library of Congress Control Number: 2008931122
ISBN-13: 978-0-7618-4170-8 (paperback : alk. paper)
ISBN-10: 0-7618-4170-9 (paperback : alk. paper)
eISBN-13: 978-0-7618-4171-5
eISBN-10: 0-7618-4171-7

♾™ The paper used in this publication meets the minimum
requirements of American National Standard for Information
Sciences—Permanence of Paper for Printed Library Materials,
ANSI Z39.48—1984

Dedication

To those who struggle.
Their thought—*our thought*—gives life the crispness and hope of a brisk October morn and offers our future the beauty of an April thaw.

Table of Contents

Acknowledgments of prior publication

Some of these poems have been published previously. In almost all cases, however, I have changed them for publication here.

Original Publication Venues

News and Letters:
Representation; 41 bullets; Like Hegel and Marx, I stand for Negation; Of time and emergence;...therefore, I am; Second Negation: Notes on the Day after the Revolution
Poems Niederngasse: The Journal of Winning Poetry. September/October 2005
The flowers and the fall
Processed World
Like a flash of darkening
Haight Ashbury Literary Journal
Calling my HMO
Journal of Progressive Human Services
Economics of welfare reform; What's a fellow gonna do?; two-two-nineteen sixty; Generation (This was my first published poem, in 1988; at that time, the journal was named *Catalyst.*)
Black Bear Review
The green, green hills of Earth; Exile; Visions of Now, Tomorrow, and Beyond; Turnpike Utopia
Lips
Victoria
Needles, drugs, and defiance: Poems to organize by
Outside . . . In; The century when hope died; Needle exchange demo, Trenton Statehouse, January 12, 1999
Paterson Literary Review
Crabs; Never Again; Second coming, with doorways
The Cancer Poetry Project Book
Sharing
Home Planet News
The spirit of America;
Murders most foul: Poems against war by a World Trade Center survivor
America; Searching; Thoughts on Manhattan streets, 9 a.m., September 20, 2002; Check out line; A Few Years Down the Road; Poem for cockroaches who glow in the dark; Our sign says "Honk if you hate war"; After, on the way to thereafter
The Ocean Grove Poetry Anthology
The apple's story
The Pedestal Magazine.com: The Political Anthology
There is no nation

Canadian Dimension
    The Old Brick Firehouse; When I was 32
Newsworks: North American Syringe Exchange Networks
    NASEC 1995 (published here as "Conferences")
Big Hammer
    Holy NASEC, April 28, 2001
Flying Horse
    Imagine #2
Arbella
    Lot's Wife Unsalted

Reprints:

Poems Niederngasse: The Journal of Winning Poetry. September/October 2005:
    Of time and emergence; Like a flash of darkening; Calling my HMO; ; Second coming, with doorways; When I was 32; Second Negation: Notes on the Day after the Revolution
Murders most foul: Poems against war by a World Trade Center survivor
    The spirit of America; There is no nation; Representation; Never again
AIDS Care
    The century when hope died; NASEC 1995 (under the title "Conferences"); Holy NASEC, April 28, 2001
Social Problems Forum: The SSSP Newsletter
    Of time and emergence; A Turnpike Utopia
Peaceful Poetry to Love Your Societal Consciousness. First Books Library
    41 bullets
Needles, drugs, and defiance: Poems to organize by
    Victoria; NASEC 1995; Imagine #2

Prizes

I rarely enter poetry contests. I have done so a few times, however; and several of these poems have won awards.

"Of time and emergence" was third prize winner, National Writers Union Poetry Contest, 2002. The judge was Adrienne Rich.

"Exile" was first prize winner of the *Black Bear Review* 2001 Poems of Social Concern Competition.

"Visions of Now, Tomorrow, and Beyond" was first prize winner of the *Black Bear Review* 1996 Poems of Social Concern Competition.

Acknowledgments of assistance

My sister, Paula Friedman, edited a literary magazine, *Open Cell*, for many years. She has given me advice about how to modify poems on many occasions. She also went through a manuscript of this book and provided many worthwhile and even brilliant suggestions. This book, and I, have gained immeasurably from her assistance.

For many years, a small group of poets met every four to six weeks to discuss our activities and to read and think about other writers' poetry. We also offered each other advice even more informally. Amanda Berry, Dutch, Tony Gruenwald, Gina Larkin and John Larkin, over the years, gave me useful insights and critiques. Gina, in particular, read through a draft of an earlier manuscript that I never published—but some of the poems from that are in this book and benefited greatly from her critique. Joe Weill, a Jersey poet of great brilliance, also gave me invaluable advice on that same manuscript.

The editors of the Raya Dunayevskaya Series on Marxism and Humanism, Kevin Anderson, Olga Domanski, and Peter Hudis, provided me with insightful advice about the Introduction to this book that helped me both to improve it and also to think through my own political history more adequately.

Introduction

This book was originally prepared for possible publication in the Raya Dunayevskaya Series in Marxism and Humanism. Although the Editors of this series approved the book for such publication, Lexington Books decided for marketing reasons to refer it to University Press of America, which accepted it as part of its Hamilton Imprint. At the suggestion of the editors of the Raya Dunavskaya series, I wrote this Introduction to present some of my own perspectives on Marxism, Marxist humanism and the problems of creating thoroughgoing social change in order to create a livable world. As a preliminary to doing this, I think I should present a few words on how I came to Marxism. Many of the events discussed below are mentioned, or in some cases animate, poems in this volume.

Unlike some of my contemporaries in the movements of the '60s, I was anything but a red diaper baby. My parents seemed uninterested in politics. One lasting imprint of my family was that it never occurred to me that I could become a full-time activist, politician, or other position focused on social change. My initial focus was on becoming a scientist and a researcher. My parents were quite happy with my ambitions to become an astronomer—an ambition that I turned away from before beginning my third year of college. At that time, based on my experiences in the movement and my sense of human needs, I decided to study economics. (Later, I went to graduate school in sociology, and got a Ph.D. in it. Later on yet, the vagaries of the job market led me to blunder into a position in AIDS research, where I have worked for over 20 years now.)

It is hard to know how I became a radical. I had no role models of radicalism around me in Washington, DC, before I entered high school, but I already had many radical ideas by then . Some of this radicalism may have come from my reading and from my thinking about the world around me. As a child who turned 10 years old in 1952, I read some of the easier-to-read emerging literature on the Nazis and the Holocaust, as well as science fiction about nuclear war and even some on futuristic corporations ruling the world directly. Before I left 6th grade, I had read Tolstoy's *War and Peace*, Steinbeck's *In Dubious Battle*, and a number of other radical novels. A college-age friend who lived across the street and was studying science gave me some of the early publications of the Atomic Scientists (who had reacted after Hiroshima and Nagasaki against the use of the atomic bomb and its threat to human existence by organizing for peace and sanity). Somehow, out of this, I began to develop a very definite belief that the world was in dire crisis and that the reigning institutions were not up to solving it.

In high school, two of my friends became active in the civil rights movement. I went with them to the Second Youth March for Integrated Schools early in 1959—which was very impressive to me and to them, since it brought 28,000 or more people to demonstrate at the Washington Monument. My friends became associated with the Washington, DC, chapter of the Congress of Racial Equality (CORE). At that time CORE was very closely affiliated with Quakerassociated war resisters and had a strong devotion to nonviolent direct action—although they only took action after torturous negotiations. When I first went to one of their meetings (sometime in the latter half of 1959, I think), they had been negotiating for some months with the downtown, all-white, YMCA to desegregate. Events, however, swept the movement forward. After the Greensboro sit-in in February, 1960 (see my poem, "two-two-nineteen sixty," in this book), I got involved in picketing a Woolworth's dime store on 14th Street. This was part of a national movement to pressure chains to desegregate their Southern stores. Later that year, CORE was part of a coalition that conducted demonstrations at Glen Echo, a large amusement park in Montgomery County, MD. This involved hundreds of people in picket lines week after week. I took part in a sit-in at Glen Echo in summer, 1960.

Then I went to college, and for the next year or so was caught up in studying math and science and in my social life. Early in my sophomore year, however, I became involved in the college peace movement, and later became involved in civil rights activities there. My involvement in the movements only increased for the rest of my college days, and then beyond that for the rest of the 1960s and the 1970s.

These movements had begun in hope. We won many victories over Jim Crow segregation, unionized many farmworkers in California, and contributed to the ending of the Vietnam War. However, as we struggled, we learned. We learned that racism was national, not just Southern; that there was such a thing as imperialism, and that US and other imperial power was helping maintain massive impoverishment and dictatorships in many "Third World" countries. We learned about the oppression of women. And as time went on, we learned that "capitalism" was deeply embroiled in all of these ills—and many others—and also that the power of capitalism was greater than the power our movements had to bring change. As we encountered these disconcerting facts, some—but by no means most—of us also learned that the problems that workers face in their lives and their workplaces meant that they were, at the very least, a powerful potential ally. Some of us took the leap from that realization to think about Marxism. I did this both through reading and through political activity.

My political activity was primary in my becoming a Marxist. Later, I will describe this and how it involved me with various strands of "Third Camp socialism" including Marxist Humanism. ("Third Camp socialism" is a term used to describe a number of organizations and strands of thought, mostly derived historically from the Trotskyist movement and the splits from it that took place in the 1940s. These saw both the US and Russian blocs as exploitative class societies. We "stood in revolutionary opposition" to the ruling classes of all those countries—and, indeed, of the entire world. It was a very healthy political stance to take, in some ways, since we never had to go through the disillusionment with various so-called socialist countries as the validity of their socialism was belied by mass action, collapse, or their instituting more American forms of capitalism from the top.)

Reading, however, was also important. Key intellectual influences on me included the works of Marx himself (particularly, at first, his letters against deterministic interpretations of his work; his Theses on Feuerbach; the first paragraphs of the Communist Manifesto where it talks about history as being the history of class struggles that result either in revolutionary change or in the mutual ruin of the contending classes; and the second and eighth paragraphs of *The 18th Brumaire* where Marx talks first about how conditions constrain human action but that humans nonetheless make their own history, and then discusses how working class revolutions get defeated only to come back again having learned from it. A trip to Europe in 1970--where I read the London *Times* quite frequently and saw that it was a mechanism through which the capitalist class mulled over its interpretations of events to its own members as well as others-- and reading Trotsky's *History of the Russian Revolution* convinced me that classes really do have reality and can act as semi-united forces. Hal Draper's *Two Souls of Socialism*, as well as ongoing discussions on the left, helped me concretize and theorize my objections to "Stalinist" societies. Sidney Hook's *Towards the Understanding of Karl Marx: A revolutionary interpretation*— although its treatment of dialectics was both inadequate and misleading, and much closer to social interactionism than to Marx or Hegel—nevertheless provided me with additional foundation about what Marxism was. It was available through the International Socialists in a bootleg edition since Hook himself refused to let it be re-published.

More important than these readings, however, was my movement experience. I learned in the movements that movements think, develop interpretations of the world and new values, argue over these interpretations and values, and grow intellectually. They do this as they try to make gains in the existing society, discover more and more realities about the existing society, and also learn about themselves, their hopes, their methods of effective action, and their limitations. Key examples of this were taking part in the Freedom movement as it went through its learning about integration, direct action, black power, and class society; and in SDS as it struggled and thought its way from left liberalism to radicalism to a mélange of viewpoints calling themselves Marxist.

Thinking is, of course, hard. It is prone to make mistakes, particularly if you do not root it in a deep philosophical understanding of what you are trying to achieve. I saw many friends in the movement get pulled off course in this way. Perhaps as a result of their not understanding that the enemy of our enemy need not be our friend, thousands of the most militant and most radical members of the movement were drawn into Maoism or other forms of "Stalinism." What happened is easy to describe, but it was a nightmare to live through and a nightmare to remember: As we came to see that the US government and capitalism were enemies of freedom and of peace, we had to think through what this meant for the movement and our goals. In the context of the movement to end the Vietnam War, it was very seductive to see the National Liberation Front of Vietnam and its allies as our friends (since they were the most visible enemies of the enemies-at-home whom we were confronting every day.) Once some members of the movement began to see the National Liberation Front of Vietnam as a friend, they began to rationalize and then to accept its ideas about struggle, leadership, and the good society. Some movement members oriented more towards the Vietnamese Communist Party or the Chinese Communist Party as "our friends;" and some oriented towards the Russian or even the Albanian Communist Party. This had tragic results. Most important, it meant that the ideas of freedom and a good world that the movement of the early sixties had begun to develop were muddled and then lost—at least among this large part of the movement—and replaced with fetishized ideas of the Party as the embodiment of truth and with seeing workers and other poor people as being unable to work out their own strategies and desires. These fetishized concepts were not well-received by the great bulk of American workers nor by most of the Black people's movement. Both groups had had too much experience of middle-class elements (and others) telling them that leadership and ideas had to come from outside or above— particularly since the clear history of the sixties was that ideas and initiative had come primarily from the (broadly conceived) Black working class and, as well, from rank-and-file labor movements that were developing ideas and struggles in opposition to union leadership bureaucracies.

This history has important implications for the current movements against the occupation of Iraq and against the new American imperialism called the "war on terrorism." It means that we need to understand that the enemy of our enemy is often our enemy. Specifically, even if we do see American imperialism and the capitalism that it expresses as our most immediate and primary enemy, this does not mean that all Iraqi resistance movements are our friends. Many of them are just as much opposed to any Marxist or humanist ideas, or even to human decency or to the needs of the planet in this age of ecological crisis, as are Bush, Halliburton, and the leadership of the Democratic Party. These Iraqi resistance movements may support theocratic rule, the subordination of women, the rule of the rich, and the suppression of "inferior" races and ethnicities just as much as does the current government of the USA—and, on some of these issues, even more so—though they lack the power to spread their wishes planet-wide. To see them as friends is to abandon what we would hope to stand for and create. Just as in the Vietnam War—when to see the National Liberation Front of Vietnam as friends led to becoming defenders of dictatorship and top-down rule and thus to losing the vision of a world of collective collaboration in which all had a say and all could take initiative—today, to see the theocratic resistance forces in Iraq, or the murderers of 9/11, as our friends will have equally devastating consequences. In both cases, what our movements need is to keep on developing our ideas of the good and our ideas of how to transform the world, and to do so around a vision of thoughts and power from below. This means that we need to work out what it means to be human and what it means to live in peace with each other and the planet—and how revolutionary struggle can actually get us *there*, to a world we want to live in. As I see it, this is the meaning of Marxism—a philosophy and way of struggle that helps workers and their potential allies and co-thinkers take over the world and re-make it to embody freedom, excitement, compassion, and a sustainable future.

Returning now to my history as part of that of the movement: In 1969, the movement was dissolving into a host of competing organizations and factions. (I analyzed this process in Friedman, "Mass Organizations and Sects in the American Student Movement and its Aftermath," *Humboldt Journal of Social Relations* 12(Fall/Winter 1984/1985): 1-24, which is a paper based on a presentation I made in 1972 that took many years to get published). At that time, as I began to develop a weak but well-grounded comprehension of Marxism, I joined a "Third Camp" organization called the International Socialists (IS). In many ways, it was the best and least sectarian of the sects that formed or found new strength at that time. As an activist, I was attracted because IS was involved effectively and responsibly in mass actions at UCLA (where I was then an assistant professor) and also had a sensible perspective on relating to workers' movements: Its worker members tried to organize rank and file movements and the rest of the organization provided support to workers' struggles as they occurred in the locality, the nation, and the world. Thus, IS members were very involved in supporting the Los Angeles component of the great Teamsters' wildcat strike of 1970 (see Friedman *Teamster Rank and File*, 1982, Columbia University Press). IS members developed many solid relationships with Teamster activists at that time; these relationships were an essential part of the process that led to the formation of Teamsters for a Democratic Union a few years later. Los Angeles IS also took part in another activity that derived in part from the 1970 Teamster wildcat--the formation *Picket Line*, an occasional newspaper that was put out by a combination of ex-student-movement Marxists and radical workers. *Picket Line* provided news and analyses of workers' struggles across unions and industries. (See Friedman, "Social Change and Rank-and-File Newspapers," *The Insurgent Sociologist* 4 (Winter, 1974): 55-57.)

It was through taking part in the broad coalition that put out *Picket Line* that I first encountered Marxist Humanist thought. Some *News & Letters* members were part of this group, and I greatly respected their comradely and honest participation in the group, and some of their ideas. Indeed, one of them sold me a subscription to *News & Letters* and I have subscribed to it for more than 30 years. On the other hand, though I respected some of their ideas and people, I was put off by what seemed to be cultish formulations about philosophy and its place in the movement; and I felt that their group had much less developed ideas about how to build a workers' movement that could defend itself and move towards power than did my colleagues in the IS. At that time, I might add, I had only the vaguest ideas about what dialectics was, and few in the IS seemed to give it much thought.

I stayed in the IS through the 1970s both in Los Angeles and after I moved to New Jersey in 1974. Throughout this time, I was part of the efforts to work with Teamster rank-and-file activists that led to the formation of Teamsters for a Democratic Union, an organization that still exists. It organizes Teamsters Union members to fight for better working conditions and lives and combines these efforts with struggles to democratize the union. I also became a rank-and-file leader in a local college chapter of the American Federation of Teachers (see "When I was 32" in the poetry section on Struggles in Our History).

I left the IS in 1979 when it went through another of its periodic splits. I did not believe that either side of the split had good ideas about what to do, and personal factors including my becoming unemployable in the academic sociology job market limited my ability (or desire) to take part in yet more internal squabbles. I thus joined neither new organization. These new entities merged to create *Solidarity* a few years later. I have worked with *Solidarity* on occasion, but I have also taken part in activities of other groups, including *News and Letters*. During the political doldrums of the 1980s, I worked on local activities in New Jersey including occupational health and safety issues, the Commoner campaign for President, and a subsequent Citizen Party race for state senate in the district where I live. I also took the lead in organizing a union at my workplace, only to be ruled out of the bargaining unit when the union was recognized. Importantly, during this time I began to think seriously about dialectics and to read C.L.R. James, *Notes on Dialectics* and the works of Raya Dunayevskaya, and to re-read some of the works of Marx and Lenin such as sections of the *1848 Manuscripts* and Lenin's *Philosophical Notebooks*. Thought and reading about dialectics had not been part of the political discussions or political approaches I had learned in the IS—to their and my detriment. At a critical point in my thinking, when I was beginning to take Hegel seriously, I was helped by an initial conversation with Kevin Anderson at his apartment in 1982.

During this period (19830, I blundered into a job in AIDS research. I have stayed in that field and in the same non-profit research organization ever since. In many ways, my ability to contribute to AIDS research and to the struggles against the spread of the virus and of sickness and death has been assisted by my ability to think dialectically and to understand the vital role of the thoughts and activities of those at the bottom of society in humanities' struggle against AIDS.

Somewhere in the mid-1980s, as I was riding a train to work on my daily commute, something about my musing and the rhythm of the train wheels inspired a poem to start itself in my head. I still have this poem (in a somewhat edited form), and re-produce it directly below:

History

All history lets me labor.
The ages of discovery—
of how to walk on two legs,
of how to shape a wheel, of how to lathe a shape—
of how the stars wheel in the heavens.

And the years of toil to build
new Gods and new theories,
ideas to direct our labor

to turn new screws, to make new words,

to build new tools
in the image of the systems that conceived them.

All history leads to the barbed wire
and thence to the Bomb.

Will our Bomb-labor negate all labor
and all history
. . .or will our labor negate the bomb?

It was the first of many—and by no means the best by a long shot, though I obviously have great fondness for it. Some of my poems are quite personal; others are quite political; still others combine the personal, the political, and sometimes sheer whimsy. I have been told that some of my poems lead readers to cry, and others inspire them to action. And some inspire people to think. Many are about struggles over AIDS prevention and care. These have been very helpful to participants in the Harm Reduction and Needle Exchange movements—as well as more broadly among AIDS researchers and doctors.

At their best, my poems are, I think, in some ways dialectical, capturing moods and thoughts and actions, showing their contradictions, enacting their negations—and maybe even being a little bit playful in the process. Or at least, this is what I tell myself on my good days . . .

In recent years, as movements have sprung up more strongly in the United States, I have been thinking more deeply about what happens after the revolution. Remembering a conversation I once had with Sam Farber, a brilliant political sociologist who was key in recruiting me to the IS in the first place, helped me see the importance of this issue. Sam suggested to me early in the 1970s that Marx's arguments against paying much attention to what would come after the revolution had become outdated and, indeed, belied by history. After Stalinism, confronting this issue was a practical necessity. I thought about that for many years, and saw (as did millions of others) that the absence of a philosophy and vision about how to re-make the world crippled and defeated movements that challenged the power of (what the IS called) the bureaucratic collectivist ruling classes in the East. This was visible in the fate of Solidarnosc in the early 1980s and has continued to this day in struggles in the former Soviet Union and Eastern Europe. This same absence, of course, visibly cripples movements in the "West" and the "South" as well.

In thinking about these issues, I realized I needed to understand the Hegelian dialectic far better than I knew it from secondary sources such as Marx, Lenin, James, or Dunayevskaya. I began reading Hegel's Encyclopedia Logic (GWF Hegel. *Hegel's Logic*, translated by William Wallace. New York: Oxford University Press, 1975). As I read, I went through the same kind of eye-opening experience that Marx and these other writers must have gone through. I saw how Hegel's impossible-to-grasp arguments opened up new understandings of history, of practice, and of action. Most important, I developed ideas about how Hegel's categories and approach could be applied to trying to understand what we will face when and if the working class (in its broad sense) actually succeeds in dispersing capitalist power and forming one or more world-embracing communal states.

I have been trying, over the last few years, to think this through in writing. I call the project the "Workers' Dialectic" project, because it is based on the insight that one should look at the dialectic from the perspective of a nascent and then transcendent workers' movement alongside the dialectic of capital. Other demands on my time make this slow going. I have published several pieces on dialectics during this period; they are listed below:

1. Friedman, Samuel R, Reid, Gary. (2002). The need for dialectical models as shown in the response to the HIV/AIDS epidemic. *International Journal of Sociology and Social Policy* 22:177-200.
2. Friedman, SR. (2005). Review of *Philosophy and Revolution: From Hegel to Sartre, and from Marx to Mao*, by Raya Dunayevskaya. *Contemporary Sociology* 34(1):77-78.
3. Friedman, SR. (2004). Review: On Darren Webb's *Marx, Marxism and Utopia. Historical Materialism* 12;2:269-280.
4. Friedman, SR. (2008). Making the World Anew in a Period of Workers' Council Rule. We! Magazine #63, Volume 2, Number 16 Wednesday, 2 April. http://www.mytown.ca/we/friedman.

In my article on "Making the world anew in the period of workers' council rule," I attempt to systematize my thoughts on this process. This article centrally posits that the post-revolutionary period will be characterized by struggle and contradiction as we try to fix up many disastrous environmental conditions left behind by capitalism, a productive apparatus predicated on the workings of the law of value, and a badly-divided working class and humanity. This working class, with its wide range of material circumstances and ideas, will have to think through and squabble over what to do when and how. It is hard to think about this post-revolutionary dialectic—but I have found that Hegel's discussion of Notion is a useful tool in speculating about what might be possible and how the limitations of the world and of each other, together with the thoughts and philosophies of workers, might structure what is possible and what needs to be done.

To end this Introduction, I will now try to set out the areas where I see myself as a Marxist Humanist and where I disagree with or have different views from the News and Letters committees as the organized expression of Marxist Humanism. First, though, I want to express my deep admiration for the efforts Marxist Humanists in the United States have been making to try to develop a vision and philosophy for the future after the revolution. I am learning a lot from what they are doing, and also from their tying it together with the question of organization. (See also Appendices 1 and 2, which express my deep debts to the thoughts of Raya Dunayevskaya and Kevin Anderson—in part, by critiquing them where I think their work can be improved upon or carried forward.) More recently, Andrew Kliman's *Reclaiming Marx's Capital: A Refutation of the Myth of Inconsistency*, published as part of the Raya Dunayevskaya Series on Marxism and Humanism, has helped me resolve questions I have had about the role of time in Marxist economics.

Most importantly, perhaps, the News & Letters Committees, which embody Marxist Humanism in the United States, impress me with their openness, honesty, courage to think about hard issues, and their grappling with dialectics. Their simple-seeming insistence that we ask about struggles how they contribute to human liberation and freedom, and to a philosophy of revolution that will have a chance of producing a decent world, is both rare and extraordinarily valuable. Their refusal to offer any scintilla of support for any movement (such as the reactionary Islamists of Iraq) just because they are fighting American imperialism, and their insistence that we work with the healthy elements of those societies that are seeking paths that could lead to freedom, is reminiscent of what originally attracted me to "Third Camp politics." *Since the News and Letters perspectives on these issues is rooted in a serious philosophy, however, it is much deeper and much more resilient than the oft-compromised approaches of the various organizations that have carried forward the International Socialist position.*

Likewise, their efforts to think through, and act on, the question of what socialism should be also corresponds with my perspective—as does their seeing Marx and Hegel and their dialectics as the philosophical basis for these thoughts and these actions. Indeed, I owe them a deep debt for helping me see the need to incorporate Hegel into my thoughts and my politics, and for pointing the way in much of their work.

On the other hand, I am less impressed with Marxist Humanists' analysis of the revolutionary process and of what the role of revolutionaries needs to be in this process. Clearly, as *News & Letters* emphasizes, one essential role is to put forward one or more liberatory philosophies of revolution that can help an insurgent and radicalizing working class to see why Margaret Thatcher's TINA argument that "There is no alternative" is false, and that its falsification in practice depends on their taking over the direction of the world.

However, it seems to me that there is another equally important task for revolutionaries to perform if we are to have revolutions develop out of revolutionary situations and thus give humanity a chance to save the world from capitalism. This is the problem of helping the working class take power— i.e., to disperse the state and to build up workers' councils of some sort as a new mode of coordination and action for the working class's own efforts to re-make social and economic reality. The failure of many working class upsurges (such as that in France in 1968, and that in Portugal in the mid-1970s) shows that the period in which revolution is possible is quite short—and, in that short period, a large section of the working class has to act to take power. In France and Portugal, and indeed in many other potential revolutionary situations, such action did not happen, and the revolution did not occur. The organization that I once was associated with, the IS, was quite clear about *its* solution to this problem. This was to form in advance a revolutionary party to act during the revolutionary crisis to win the working class away from reformist and half-way views and help workers organize to have their (newly-formed) workers councils take power. As a prerequisite to succeed at this task, the party would have to have been deeply involved in working class and other struggles in the years leading up to the revolutionary situation and to have earned respect among wide numbers of workers, including many who disagreed with its revolutionary conclusions. I might add that both the form of this party and the ways it should act to gain support and respect were topics of rather healthy debate in the organization for the first 5 or 6 years I was involved with the IS—and that rancorous and unresolved disagreements on what should be done were part of a process that degraded both debate and solidarity and that led me to leave the IS and its successor organizations.

I agree with *aspects* of the underlying argument the IS made at that time— there is a need for one or more groups of revolutionaries with wide support among worker activists to take a clear revolutionary stance in the workers councils, and to win the councils and a large part of the class as a whole to disperse the bourgeois state and to take power. Further, they have to do this in a brief time frame. This, however, is not the same as saying that a revolutionary party is needed, since I strongly suspect we will have (and need) a number of truly revolutionary groups with solid working class support—and that their mutual criticisms, together with their active cooperation in pushing the revolution towards dispersing the capitalist state and setting up new forms of coordination and power, will be essential to a successful revolution and then to successful transformation human society and life.

Furthermore, the history of the IS, its splits, and its efforts since then (in Solidarity and the International Socialist Organization) shows me that their answers to the question of "how to do it" were not sufficient to enable them to weather the political reaction of the 1980s and since very successfully. The specific history behind the splits also convinces me that any version of the Trotskyist "party to lead" cannot succeed. (Neither can the Stalinist or Maoist versions—which are clearly on the other side of the class line in that they are ways to organize a new state that would exploit the working class and the Earth in unsustainable ways.) Indeed, the ambivalent and only-partial break of the US International Socialists with Trotsky's thought (particularly given the embrace of Trotsky by the much larger British component of this tendency), and its failure to ground this partial break philosophically, contrasts woefully with News and Letters' clear understanding that Trotsky failed to develop a viable dialectic and that this failure has been the ground for many of the failures of Trotskyist formations over the last half century and more.

Thus, I am left seeing two interacting roles for revolutionaries and for revolutionary organizations: To put forward philosophies of the revolution and of the future; and to work successfully during the revolutionary situation to win the working class to take power. Marxist Humanism has made considerable strides on the first question, and I like to think that my Workers' Dialectic project will make a contribution to that (along with my poetry—see the section of my poetry entitled Notion: Making the World Anew.) However, the dialectic of winning the worker class to take power, and its organizational requisites, is a more important part of the dialectic of organization and philosophy than Marxist Humanist leaders seem to think. I freely admit that I do not have an answer to how to create such a comprehensive dialectic in thought and actions. But I do think that it is necessary to pose *this* question of transformative philosophies and socially-grounded action, as the dialectical question—a question that may be seen as merging the "practical Idea" and the "theoretical Idea." (See Appendix 2: Sam Friedman, Notes on the Practical Idea and the Russian Revolution: A letter of commentary on *Lenin, Hegel, and Western Marxism. News and Letters,* July, 1996, for more discussion of this). Solving this question seems to be an essential part of our revolutionary task.

What is this task? Nothing less than to help save humanity and the world from capital and its depredations, and to make a new world in which we can struggle with one another on the shape of an Earth in which ecological disaster has been staved off and we can live in freely developing liberation, freedom, compassion, and creativity. One vision of what this might be like in the early years is given in my poem "After, on the way to thereafter," in Part 3 of this book (Notion: Making the World Anew). It is my earnest hope that some of the readers of this book may help to create this world and to embody this vision in a much more concrete and more pleasing world than I can now foresee.

Being: Loving and living through the daily grind

Accumulate, accumulate! That is Moses and the prophets! (Karl Marx, *Capital*, Volume 1, chapter 24)

The greater the social wealth, the functioning capital, the extent and energy of its growth, and, therefore, also the absolute mass of the proletariat and the productiveness of its labour, the greater is the industrial reserve army. . . . The more extensive, finally, the lazarus-layers of the working-class, and the industrial reserve army, the greater is official pauperism. *This is the absolute general law of capitalist accumulation. . . .*

It follows therefore that in proportion as capital accumulates, the lot of the labourer, be his payment high or low, must grow worse. (Karl Marx, *Capital*, Volume 1, chapter 25)

Work and Daily Life

OF TIME AND EMERGENCE

While honored Scholars seminar about
varying Perceptions of Time,
the sociolinguistics of emergent boundaries,
Culture as a proper noun,
and the semiotic implications of Coca-Cola and porcelain
as signifiers of post-modern identity,
they sip colas from cans stamped by mechanics
whose days are orchestrated
by a Charlie Chaplin on speed,
colas lugged up the stairways of Academe
by herniated drivers whose kidneys are bruised daily
by suspensionless trucks rushing through potholed New Brunswick streets,
through streets where unscheduled teens chase Time
in 15-minute repetitions of syringe-assisted chemical culture,
while their mothers' sponges tap out the rhythm
of the hours before shift's end
on ever-glistening porcelain toilet-bowls awaiting corporate asses,
and their fathers do Time within boundaries
of moldy cement, do seconds, do minutes, do months, seasons, years,
indeed decades of Time
before they can themselves be emergent from boundaries,
can walk past potholes
to beg a cola, a job, a mop,
and carcinogenic solvents
to scour the floors of each seminar room
once a semester
lest moldy post-modern musings
comprehend need and its angers,
lest they mutate into ideas
of freedom for
all.

LIKE A FLASH OF DARKENING

Like a flash of darkening
in a naively blue sky
an offhand slur
from a minor-league boss
transforms my mood
and my digestion.

A sidewise sneer, a careless word,
a memo with the lightest criticism,
and years of rage
at the structured insult
that is my life
spew steam like surging espresso.

Nights of heartburn.

Thunderous fantasies.

As my teeth shatter like falling teacups
from my stifling, gritting rage
our noble superiors
stalk the world
like the dinosaurs they are,
unaware,
self-centered,
liberal,
trampling unseen personas

underfoot.

CALLING MY HMO

6:33 on a June morning in Vancouver,
sun turning on the clouds,
the phone answers in 9:33 a.m. New Jersey:
"This call may be
recorded
for educational purposes
and for quality control."
Then a click,
and the recorded voice intones
"All the client advocates are busy.
Please wait,"
and the Muzak starts,
broken every minute or two
as the recorded voice intones,
"An advocate will be with you shortly,"
click,
more Muzak.

6:58, as the recorded voice intones,
the clouds have grown thicker,
the music is maintaining itself well.
My image of the advocates grows ever more manic,
one or two underpaid people
with eight phone lines
wired into their heads
taking care of business,
giving maintenance to the business
that talks about health,
tapes their conversations
with hundreds of folks like me
whose muttered curses are taped
(while the Muzak plays on)
to provide soundtrack and laughter
for stockholders' meetings
as we get maintained in our lives only
by knowing that Quality Control
will get royally pissed
if we die on the line.

7:01. The clouds have now grown menacing.
The sunlight has not maintained itself.
I think "half an hour on the line,
time to hang up,"

when a pleasant voice comes on the line.
We talk cheerily about business.
When I describe this poem,
she dares not laugh.

THE FLOWERS AND THE FALL

Every spring, to the raucous cheers of returning geese,
J&J, the megacorp of New Brunswick,
plants flowers anew
on my morning commute.
This year, it was thousands of red begonias,
petals dextrous as fingers manufacturing band-aids,
and towering elephant ears
as fortresses over the garden-plot.
Every morning and evening through the months of light,
they waved good evening to my home-walking grin,
or good morning to my retreating back.
But when the day of goblins had passed,
its trick-or-treat children cheering the return of night,
and these floral workers in the garden of megacorp
had passed their prime,
their beauty sinking like a 32-year-old temp's,
the megacorp outsourced shovels.
Begonias and elephant ears got downsized,
red and green presents
for the pre-Christmas scrap heap.
No early retirement,
no rusting trailers near Florida swamps,
no bingo afternoons,
no channel-surfing nights.
One day, my commuter's walk
waved floral greetings.
The next, empty soil,
arid as a balance sheet,
as a future of corporate plans.

SECOND COMING, WITH DOORWAYS

When the trumpet of the second coming
blared like a car outside the door
in the hands of a horny date, crying
"Welcome to the New Millennium,"
promising salvation,
promising joy,
and as the oppressed stirred,
pulses beating,
hearing freedom, hearing release,
bosses locked the world's doorways
like the Triangle Shirtwaist Company
or the chicken-plucking-plant
down South,
mumbled about orders to meet,
production,
profits,
never acknowledging
the fires to come.

MODERN TIMES

We sell our lives,
hour by hour,
task by task,
wrinkled brow by downturned mouth,
year after year from striding, grinning morning
to limping afternoon
and to an evening of looking backwards
at decades of disappointments,
occasional sunny glades of battles won
or battles lost,
but at least battles *fought*,
rather than the slow oozing of life
sand-drop by blood-drop, hour by decade,
for pennies, dimes, and dollars,
selling our life's time for dreams of retiring
until the gold watch chimes the hour
of our worklife's finale
and our arthritic legs walk the walk
of freedom regained,
limping a few last weeks with head erect
before our shrunken wrinkled moon
goes down
forever.

AIDS in an Indifferent World

As an AIDS researcher, I agonize over AIDS and the struggles we have had to wage to get any action at all from the US government around effective prevention and around making sure that people who need medicine have access to it. Thus, these poems are "work poems" for me.

IN THE COURSE OF HUMAN EVENTS

> When in the Course of human events, it becomes necessary for one people to dissolve the political bands which have connected them with another, and to assume among the powers of the earth, the separate and equal station to which the Laws of Nature and of Nature's God entitle them, a decent respect to the opinions of mankind requires that they should declare the causes which impel them to the separation.
>
> *Revolutionary manifesto by the Continental Congress, July, 1776*

Like the plagues that devastated Europe past,
AIDS now tests beliefs,
institutions of production and exchange,
the legitimacy of all power,
and justifications for a world
of states--armed to destroy.

As the Black Death challenged
reigning religions and princes' justice,
and as European bacteria
laid low empires and gods
West of the Atlantic,
our modern plague provokes
questions of fire,
questions of revolt:

Why do medications abound only
where the virus does not?
Why does prevention provoke resistance
from the wealthy with the power,
from the country with the bombs?
Why are cutbacks demanded,
hospitals closed,
public health defunded,
so investors can run free?
When, in the course of human events,
can our health matter?
Our safety be?

THE PLAGUE OF TIME

In the year that PATCO died
loved by few, decried, despised,
in that year, a year of woe,
AIDS was found, so long ago.

As jobs were lost, evictions boomed,
farms closed down, the virus found,
Contras killing, virus teeming,
the rich stayed wealthy, others doomed.

Twenty years have passed, have gone,
babies born, who died forlorn,
corporate mergers spread like virus,
years of tears, ears of sighs.

Our unions weak, our lives ignored,
like many friends who shrank and died,
since AIDS was found, so long ago,
so many years of wasted time,

      to bloat

      their blasted

      bottom

      line.

VICTORIA

The Spanish sun stares like a giant flashbulb too stubborn to turn itself off,
the baked walls beam heat into our blasted eyes,
but offer the solace of winding shadows
to me and to Victoria.

We climb upwards through the narrow streets of Toledo,
famous through the cruel centuries for sharpened steel and hardened blades,
for incisive Islamic and Sephardic scholars
and for its Inquisition of heated steel and sharpened flames
that brought ethnic purity to the hills of La Mancha.

We clamber over the small black round paving stones
that line the streets of this Spanish oven,
stones worn smooth by the boots of Don Quixote
and the ass of Sancho Panza,
scurried over for centuries by rats and their plague-bearing fleas,
and by doctors with no help to give
            but to urge faith in God's goodness
            and the Holy Inquisition,
and we talk idly of AIDS.

Over lunch, we chew the food of La Mancha
beneath the walls of Alcazar,
the fascist fortress that graces
the peak of Toledo,
where the forces of their God, their manliness
and proper authority
gave their "Todo por la Patria."

To her, this land is home.
Her friends coughed Pneumocystis
in the hospitals of Madrid
while the Social Democratic heirs of the caudillos,
            and the Inquisition
viewed the dying of drogaddictos
as irrigation for a baking land,
and crucified her efforts to stem the spread
of plague reborn.

To me, the land is foreign.
My eyes, sunblasted, see the bravery of Barcelona,
            of its workers who defied Franco and the world
            to build a life which people could run themselves, where

daily need would rule, not God, not profits,
in the tired, flashing eyes, lisping words, and lonely battles
of this 90 pound woman.

OUTSIDE ... IN

Sitting in the lightless cavern that was my office
in the hate-ridden spring of 1987,
when "Just say No" was the mantra from above
and the message for users was "Enter treatment or die,"
with death clearly the hoped-for choice.

My employers were more humane,
they really wanted folks to enter treatment,
piss into cups every few days to prove their troth,
slurp their methadone under watchful eyes
or go through headfixing at a TC uptown, downtown, uptime, downtime.
So sorry if you get HIV, but treatment is our business,
not condoms, not bleach, and certainly not
the exchange of needles.

Sitting in my gloomy office, mulling inertia, hatred, callous systems,
hearing the phone ringing,
picking it up wondering "What is it this time?"
Another Assistant D.A. seeking quotes to distort
for the papers?
Or more work, more requests, more denunciations of the helpless?

I muttered, "Yeah . . . what is it?"
or maybe "Hello,"
heard a gentle voice, quiet steel, in return,
"Hello. This is Kathy Oliver calling,
from Portland, Oregon.
I hear you might know something
about giving drug users needles
to prevent AIDS."

My mind flashed joy like a salmon
leaping under a rainbowed sky,
or like the April sunlight in 1961 when my first Massachusetts winter
broke into icicles dripping sparkling water
that sang its way through the slush that was Cambridge sidewalks,
or like the proverbial Western movie
when the cavalry sweeps over the hill bringing salvation
(even though they really brought death, racist eviction, and even smallpox
in the American rehearsal
of the Negro removal that is modern-day AIDS).

But here was the telephone,

me beaming in my windowless office,
talking to salvation,
talking needles,
talking life.

Ecology: The Whole World at Risk

The crisis of the environment may well end human history. These poems speak both to that fact and also to some ways pollution and global warming have brought grief into my life and that of the world in recent years.

THE GREEN, GREEN HILLS OF EARTH

As my train creeps by the landfills
built on the swamps that once bred
reeds, mosquitoes, and frogs
to mingle amid opalescent mud
perfumed by the resins and metallic salts
of Jersey industry,
I remember the years of trucks dumping debris,
of trucks climbing the cliffs of compacted residues
to dump their loads
and clamber slowly downwards,
their drivers hidden from the thoughts of commuters
but not from the supercharged air,
supercharged air through which gulls soared
to confetti the sky and the slowly-rising hills
in their wing-driven hunger.

Today, the hills sport grass and dandelions,
a lawn broken by scattered leafy trees,
as nature's heartiest species flout once again
their guerilla presence
despite the chemical woes
wreaked on a reeking Earth
by the drive for profits and corporate survival.

Long after I die,
long after you and I are long forgotten,
long after Bergen-Belsen, My Lai, the Disney Corporation
and even Love Canal
are the merest footnotes in historical monographs
that nobody reads,
these hills will remain.

These hills will remain.
Children will run laughing up and down
their grassy slopes
(where once drivers without spacesuits
drove up and down
up and down, dump and load,
dump the load).
Children, smiling,
will climb trees,
dig mud pies,
toss mud into the sky

and each others' hair,
smell the dandelions,
and lie on the grassy lawn
while chewing the green, round stems,
one with their eternal Earth,
one with the hills they will praise as having lasted forever,
growing cancers
for ten thousand years.

CRABS

I was born late on a July afternoon
into a war-torn world
   under the sign
   of Cancer the Crab.

Did my father gaze that night into the starry Richmond sky?
   I can never know --
   but if he did, I do know one thing:
   He did not see Cancer blinking back.

As a child, I had two passions.
I loved the stars,
spent hours looking upwards
or staring down into the eyepiece of my telescope,
tracing constellations bright or faint,
awestruck at the beauty of Praesepe,
the sparkling jewels in the heart of the Crab.

Crabs were my other passion,
steamy, spicy, fat-drenched slivers of crustacean sensuality.
I tore their shells off their backs, smashed their claws,
sucked their flesh;
and my parents, sister, and cat
joined in a communal gluttony of savory satisfaction.

When I grew up,
I left the dark nights and crustacean waters
of the Potomac basin
far behind,
and moved north; then west; and west again.

Under skies rarely clear,
where I never saw that zodiacal crab
through the smog and the neon,
I answered the telephone.
It was my uncle.
"Cancer," he said.
And so I lost my mother
to the crab's grasping claws
and the avid smoking of the Flapper generation.

Now, we are besieged anew by these monstrous, crabby cells.
This time they are after my daughter.

We expect to smash them with chemical slaughter,
        to destroy them now and forever,
but we do not KNOW.

As we lay out plans, devise strategies of attack,
        and keep our hopes up with statistics and love,
I think about the cancerous Zodiacal sign
        that has filled my years,
and I wonder why I could not have been beset
by bulls, lions, scorpions – or even virgins.

SHARING

I have joined my daughter in a new language,
feelings,
tastes:
the slicing of the biopsy blade,
sipping barium sulfate,
nervous ounce after nervous ounces,
iodine flickering metallic on empty tongues,
the horizontal dance through the doughnut
as the CAT scans intestines, vessels, fates.

We have each been invited to the ball
by the big empty.
We have each stepped back for the nonce,
back from that dance, from the lilting tempos
of Mr. Bones.

REAL ESTATE

Trees stretch their limbs black
against the blue pre-sunrise sky
on this hilltop where I live.
As I walk down the blocks
towards the river-bridge
30 miles from the ocean shore,
I wonder when the wave-lines
will stretch to where.
Here is Aaron's home,
where this peacenik mathematician reads histories
of the decline of civilizations.
To reach his door, I must climb
six feet or so of stairs.
When will the waves tickle
the street before them?
When will they moisten his lawn,
mildew his rugs,
submerge his roof?

Every day I take the train to Manhattan,
a train atop rails that soon will be soccer fields
for gamboling crabs.
I emerge from railed tunnels to a Penn Station
whose Madison Square Garden may see
dolphins parade in victory
at their conquest of this land.

As I ride the elevator to my office,
seven stories up,
I fantasize about commuting by motorboat,
oceanfront doorstep to water-girt windowsill,
maybe fishing from my office
hoping for some bass or flounder
while hoping against hope
my hook doesn't snag
some remnant bones from the ruins
of Katrinas yet to come.

THE POWER OF LOVE AGAINST

When Katrina sent its waters
all the government gave was orders,
save the rich and leave the poor,
let the Jefferson Parish Ku Klux Kops
shoot those fleeing, to make them stop.
Tell the soldiers, "shoot to kill,"
keep out friends,
veterans
or whoever has the will
to bring help to any people
the government loves to hate,
to ban help from New Orleans
until it's far too late.

> The talents of the workers
> against the goals of the rich folks' state,
> the power of love for others
> against the arrogant power of hate.

When the government sent its orders,
"Let Black people rot and die,"
then the veterans from Camp Casey, and from the whole U.S. of A.,
gathered as the people...as truckers, nurses, givers—
to do what the rich man's government wouldn't,
to do what a rich man's government couldn't,
to give the dying succor,
to give the dying life,
to give love to those the government
gives only hatred, ruin and strife.

> The talents of the workers
> against the goals of the rich folks' state,
> the power of love for others
> against the arrogant power of hate.

So it's time to make a stand now,
Not tomorrow, but today,
they want to steal our land,
to drive New Orleans' poor away.
Their TV shows echo only thoughts
of profit from disaster,
and the rich folks' urgent need
to erase from all our minds

the meaning of Katrina:
that when disaster
demonstrated
the hatred of the state,
we, the people, delivered aid
to people left to rot and die;
that we, the people,
have the power
to make a land where all help all,
so we can crush their hatred,
their lying and their laws.

      The talents of the workers
      against the goals of the rich folks' state,
      the power of love for others
      against the arrogant power of hate.

MILLENNIUM

A thousand years ago,
mathematics prospered algebraically
and poetry and art spoke to pomegranates
in Arabia, Palestine, Africa, and Iberia.
Savage braggarts in rusty iron
quarreled through European swamps,
killing for titles to the land and toil of the tethered many.
Sailors blundered through northern seas,
touching upon America
with but little result
since its red Americans were more civilized,
more culturally competent,
more ecologically adept
than the interlopers from a Europe
of neighborhood wars.
Children were born to die diseased
or live with eyes bent to the soil,
digging, stirring, planting, reaping
from early childhood to early dying.
The skies were clear, the air unpolluted,
the water clear of chemical poisons
though replete with bacteria
of the human gut.

A thousand years have cleared Northern waters
of the bacteria
but filled water, air, soil, and bodies,
North and South,
with industrial waste, airplanes, and electronic signals
from satellites far above.

Forty or fifty generations,
thousands of wars, millions of species departed,
billions of exploited, painful lives,
our creation through this millennium past.

The warming earth shivers,
globally awaiting
millennium next.

Imperial Power in Action

Many of these poems appeared in a pamphlet of my work, published in 2005 by a local peace group I have been active in, the Central Jersey Coalition against Endless War. That pamphlet is *Murders most foul: Poems against war by a World Trade Center survivor.*

THE SPIRIT OF AMERICA

I talked with the spirit of America last night,
in a bar on Lower Broadway.
He was glib and bombastic,
macho, violent, but kind,
wearing an ornate yellow ribbon,
and clothed in red,
white,
and blue.
Yellow, for the golden bubbling beer
that filled his cup and his mouth
with diatribes and tremulous boasting
of yellow, craven Iraqis
fleeing the turkey shoot on
yellow sands.
Red, then, for his eyes,
and his nose,
and for sunset shots of bloodshot cities.
White for the foam and the shining suns
of boyhood summers
steeped in brew and racial pride,
and for the bandages he sent
to the victims of every earthquake or raging fire.

And blue? for the Blues,
for the hollowed veins of the users sleeping outside the bar, and
for the blue-blooded party goers
oblivious in their limos
as they pass the junkies,
me,
and my conflicted companion.

AMERICA

Others
exist
for our pleasure,
their lands
ours
to explore,
mine,
pump,
or plant
with
seeds
that Others
must
grow
so we can eat—

or ours to plant
with
bombs
dropped
from
our
sky.

Others
can labor,

or
Others
can die.

THE APPLE'S STORY

Eve's apple
grew back its bitten arc,
grew legs to travel,
left Eden in a huff
at that woman's rejection
after just one loving bite.
It bummed around the seedy parts
of a verdant globe.
After a few thousand years,
it built up its self-respect,
climbed back into a tree,
hoping to get chosen again,
become part of a fine pie—or an English cider.
But no one picked it
for even one tasty teensy nip,
so that forlorn apple just kept on hanging from its aging tree year after year,
'til finally, in a bitter spite, that hangdog apple threw itself at a thinker's head
dozing below—
but missing its aim, it did not conk,
but simply
inspired
theories of gravitation,
the orbits of missiles,
and their graceful Falls.

One apple.
Two seekers of knowledge.
Hundreds of missiles.

Billions of apples
baked in their trees.

BROKEN HOME

> To Rachel Corrie and other volunteers
> who risk their lives to defend
> Palestinian homes and people
> from the Israeli bulldozer

I tap my catnip mouse
under the shattered chair.
He stroked my fur their last night
as my insides stoked purr
and my claws worshipped His
mother-warm lap.
His hand rubbed my head,
and He spoke softly of His love for His land,
then returned to writing,
writing a love poem
to this ancient house.
His family had lived here
six hundred years.

I walk to the splintered cupboard,
eat from a splattered bag,
and return under my chair to huddle anew
beside his cooling hand and crushed red-wet lap,
and I wonder who promised us to the bulldozers?
who lets them smash us
on our spoken-for land?

THERE IS NO NATION

GW Bush, Jr., November 6, 2001:
"You're either with us or against us
in the fight against terror."

Flags furled forth across America
after the Towers burned, crumbled, collapsed,
flags as symbols of "us," of our mystic unity.
And the fruits of this unity shone forth
in the hallowed American Way:
15 billion dollars for the victimized
airlines
who showed American Unity in action,
passing on pink slips, tens of thousands of pink slips,
in patriotic unity, unity with their workers—
from whom they disunited.

Unity rang forth from the lips
of the talking heads,
mouths of the few
who own networks, rule airwaves.
And musicians, cartoonists, whoever
asked even the least of questions
received patriotic pink slips of their very own.

Signs proclaimed "United We Stand"
in brilliant red, white, and blue,
but as the welfare moms ran down
their 5 year lifetime limit,
facing starvation in a pink-slip nation,
their nation's leader said nothing
about unity with them,
or with any in need.
He thundered instead for revenge,
for tax cuts for his wealthy friends,
for unity indeed.

The militant wing of the "us" of the nation,
the skulking Kluxers and their pals in tax-wealthy weapons labs,
sent a gift to the nation,
anthraxed love letters to "lefty" liberals
whose leftness escapes detection
and whose liberality extends only to tax cuts.
And again, the nation rose to the challenge

in a traditional American Way,
with investigations, doctors, and evacuations
for the powerful,
smart bombs for the scapegoated Afghans
who had sent no letters through the mail,
and benign neglect and orders to "keep on sorting"
for each postal worker with rotting, anthraxed lungs.

REPRESENTATION

A Rutgers crew rests in the Raritan
on the morning after
the President's speech
on Abu Ghraib.
As the President said,
prison torture
"does not represent the America
I
know,"
nor that of the happy collegians rowing
upstream.

But those in the cellblocks of Pennsylvania
and Virginia where soldiers Graner and Frederick
learned to "guard,"
and those in Parchman or Coahoma County
down in Mississippi
both then and now,
and the INS detainees
of Elizabeth, New Jersey,
and throughout the land—all know,
all have seen the beatings
and suffered the sensory deprivation—
and all have whispered these truths
when outside
so their neighbors have heard
these words,
these truths.

So ask not those upstream
about
torture,
about
prisons,
but forgive them not
for they choose not to
know.

THOUGHTS ON MANHATTAN STREETS, 9 A.M., SEPTEMBER 20, 2002

Hundreds of innocent people
walk from the train station
to toil their eight hours
at everyday jobs,
to earn everyday paychecks.
Across this city of stricken Towers,
millions of innocent people
walk from subways or cars
to toil their hours,
to earn their pay.
As do millions more,
innocents all,
across this land of re-shaped plains.
Millions walk to their jobs,
toil their hours,
earn their pay.
Their labor makes products,
tapes films,
discovers new ways.
Together, innocents all,
we enrich our bosses
and empower our rulers
to hire our innocent children
when they are grown at last,
to hire these innocent children
of us innocent parents
who walk from our subways or cars,
who toil for our paychecks,
who raise our children
as innocents to be hired
to fly planes,
to push buttons or triggers
to kill other children
whose innocent parents walk
to earn everyday paychecks
at everyday jobs
somewhere beneath,
beneath our compassion
our compassion,
perhaps in Korea,
perhaps in Iraq.

CHECK OUT LINE

Today is grocery day
in Year Nine of the War
As I reach the line's front,
the checkers take my loyalty card
so I can get low low discounted prices
like the loyal customer I am
and so President Ashcroft can be sure
I am buying Wheaties,
Coca Cola,
"Kill an Infidel" comic books,
the Bible plaque of the day
and loin of terrorist
for my red-blooded American roast.

When the scanner beeps,
the voices yell
"Hands on your head, traitor scumbag!
I mean you!
Hands on your head and spread them,
traitor scumbag."

As I was dragged from the Shop and Drop,
asking why? what had I done?
they said my loyalty card
wasn't doing its duty,
didn't buy enough gas
for two SUVs,
a snowmobile,
and other necessities
any loyal American
had to have,
and they didn't listen when I cried,
"But I'm on Social Security!
I can only afford to drive a quarter gallon a week,
that's twelve dollars right there!"

But they didn't listen,
didn't care,
those checkers
at the check-out line.

Yarra River at Southbank Mall, Melbourne, Australia

Wurundjeri kids may once have played
along this riverbank now hedged
with railroad tracks,
Wurundjeri kids may once have viewed white folks seize their playlands,
seen sabers flailing,
seen parent's sundered heads
soccer balls on their field of play,
or felt whips or rifle-butts
on straining backs.

Today, domes, spires, oblong Towers, and a clock on concrete
fill my view.
A club of elders cycles chatting by
While shop workers inhale breezes and ciggies
On their morning break.

No hint of sabers, whips or rifle-butts taints
today's idyllic air.

Tonight, as the conference opens to discuss
reducing drug-related harm,
the speakers will recognize the traditional owners of this now-Australian land—
an act unthinkable in my America
where similar terrorist thefts
pass unremarked.

The corpses know not the difference--
and their descendants live no longer
on these blessed, watered soils.

NEVER AGAIN

Red stains the walls of the mosque of proud Hebron,
red on the floor and red on the ceiling,
as rage blossoms red in the hearts of the people,
but no anger remains in the eyes on the floor.

Some claim it was done by a single lone madman,
a nut born in Brooklyn, New York, USA,
who used a machine gun in red-anger fury,
or maybe in justice avenging his friend,

but the eyes on the floor knew instants of horror
at the guards who stood silent, who chose not to come,
as they honored the status of Jews as too godlike
to be bothered or shot at as they murdered their prey.

And fear rises yet in the hearts of the victims,
the Arabs whose lovers lie dead in the dust,
treated as servants or as rugs to be trod on,
or roaches to slaughter in a moment of whim.

And the blood in the mosque cries wildly for wisdom,
and the barbed wire walls wail wildly for love,
while the fear and the hate and the loathing of killers
remind us that evil demands total change.

When millions of Jews filled the ovens in Poland,
then Roosevelt abandoned their lives and their pain,
turned refugees back, overseas to be slaughtered,
gave Hitler free passage for his railroads of doom,

but the survivors' grown children now dress up as statesmen,
and they arm the grandchildren with weapons of war,
and plant them as guardsmen for orchards and temples,
and watch as their sons strut like Nazis reborn.

But the eyes on the floor reflect on these questions:
"Why do the tortured now torture others?
how can their children turn into wolves?
who will negate their power and fears?"

The lips of the dead ask these questions of strangers,
questions now written in blood on the floor:
"Who pays for these weapons? finances the bombers?
Who profits from lives which we spent in the dust?"

Repression and Oppression

In thousands of direct and indirect ways, power and disdain shape our lives. These range from the slights, sneers and hardships that the oppressed encounter every day, to the guns and clubs of police, and to lynchings and other murders by those enacting power-entrenched hatred.

LOT'S WIFE UNSALTED

When my tears finally returned
to irrigate my freeze-dried body,
Sodom had vanished,
"Sinland" emerged,
a post-Disney pro-creation
of family values
offering roller-coaster rides through avenues afire,
a tunnel of by-gone debauchery,
and a video of me,
of a wife never named
who neglected her children for books,
who read history as butcheries in the name of God,
who inspired women to make love, not whore,
a woman who clearly deserved the wrath,
a sexy nameless sinner whose sinuous saline body shrivels
in a video-taped epic of God's justice
into a pillar of non-kosher salami.

But after I emerged re-baptized
by my body's sensuous juices,
after the obligatory tour of Sinland,
endless interviews by strutting heads,
and a fortune collected from the A.M.A.
for my endorsement of iodized salt,
I returned to history, to books,
to looking backwards to look ahead,
to urging my neighbors
to script their lives as poetry,
to think, to feel, to rejoice,
not to live or to die as sacrificed virginities
but to work together against war,
against chastity belts, against Gucci-clad Godlets
who posit cutbacks as necessity,
offering only arid eons
as dusty as my desert years.

This poem is dedicated to Liz Dean for her suggesting a brilliant re-framing of a
prior poem

MISSISSIPPI HANGING

We are a land of progress,
almost everyone agrees,
for there are no longer lynchings
from Mississippi's trees.

So Roy Veal dangled, hanging,
from a tree-entangled rope,
but it couldn't be a lynching
just one man who couldn't cope.

No, it couldn't be a lynching,
the Wilkinson County sheriff said—
black Sheriff Jackson said—
so it's suicide instead;

the doc found no abrasion
no contusions, no duress,
so suicide's the verdict,
there's no torture, just distress;

he was a man of weakness,
poor Roy Veal just couldn't cope,
so he hanged himself from his tree-limb
with self-inflicted rope.

Or was it rich folks' justice?
Was it just White folks' law?
The greed of White landowners
who grasp for more and more?

They coveted hiss trees for lumber,
claimed to own his family's land,
with a cash-and-power lawsuit
to back up their demands.

And since it's rich folks' justice,
for damages they sued,
for 18 thousand dollars,
Veal's land, and his forest, too.

So white folks' just-us fingers
may not have held his rope,
merely their rich white justice
lynched his family, land, and hope.

CATHARSIS IN BLUE

They call it justice
when the perp goes down,
the blue-uniformed avenger seizes the junkie,
the judge numbers her years,
the iron gate clangs shut,
and her hands grip the bars
as the ads for cat chow begin,
cinematic clichés of cleansing catharsis,
the show concluded,
the world made right.

But pot-bellied children and rib-limned cats still squabble
over bits of Purina,
dark skins still cringe at jeering threats
or bruise from the beatings
by sainted heroes in blue,
and Blue Monday universalizes
in a world of "No Alternative"
'til the anxiety at the gateway
to the office, the mill, the studio
spreads from Monday morning to afternoon,
stains Tuesday and Wednesday,
deluges Thursday in blue waters,
drowns TGIF
and trickles through the weekend,
a life of Blue Mondays,
of gateways clanging behind you,
so you flee to fables of falling perps
and a world where some evils—
ANY evils—
last not lifelong.

41 BULLETS

In an America mesmerized
by fantasies of soaring stocks
and of heroic police saving lives,
bursting villains,
41 bullets punctured the flesh of Amadou Diallo,
home at the doorway to his Bronx apartment,
41 bullets red-splashed how cops serve and protect
blacks,
workers,
immigrants,
life
so the eyeballs of America had to see,

just as cops' bullets have torn flesh and terminated souls for decades,
displaying a "just-us" for all to see
but soon forgotten
by the television and newspapers of the bottom line
always defended by cops and their guns.

In Memoriam, Matthew Shephard

The winds were so cold
on the blood on his face,
the ropes rubbed his bone
under raw country sky,
the hours of night
crept like eons of pain,
while his killers exalted
their hatred as God's.

When the gays of New York
joined other mad mourners
in a march through the streets
with tear-drops and rage,
the cops, like the fiends
who tied Matthew to death,
used clubs and arrests
to enforce their law's order:
No tears and no anger
that upset the profits
of commerce;
no sorrow allowed
except on command.

Same Thing, Different Forms

As I discussed in the Introduction, it was very painful to me personally, and very harmful for the movements of the sixties, when many friends who were part of the movement changed into apologists for dictatorships under the pressures of the logic of "the enemy of my enemy is my friend" and/or after becoming convinced that true radicalism resided in "the Party."

It is once again painful to see some of the "left" orienting towards the theocratic wing of the resistance to imperialism in Islamic lands.

Some of my poetry—perhaps too little, but I have only limited control over my Muse—reflects my anguish at these events.

UNCLE JOE

Like Hamlet on his eerie walk,
I chatted with a ghost last night,
the ghost of Judas Willy.
Stalin's uniform shone like a pearl
under an ashen moon
and the red star on his cap blazed
like Antares
in the heart of *its* scorpion.

"Sam," he explained,
"when I walk weary through the hills
of my old Georgian home,
gunshots, greed, and hatred
surround me
as its native sons
fight over the mess
my heirs created.
And the domes and cellars of modern Moscow
lack the discipline and devotion
of the days of my glory,
when we buried the last hold-outs
of our youthful dreams of a world
without profits, without bosses, a world of equals,
in the slaughters of peasants and workers who did not
know their place,
and then showed the world and the Germans
that we too could fight
for our dachas, our limos, and our rule."

And he puffed his pearly-hued pipe
and filled the pre-dawn mist
with curling smoke,
and told of his admiration for this new guy,
who knew what he stood for,
what Uncle Joe had always stood for –
wealth for those with talent,
law and order,
and cheerful obedience –
though he confided his worries that Boris and his cronies
might be too soft to make it stick.

A blue jay began its morning prayer,
and was joined by another,
by a whole chorus of birds and crickets
sounding their joy
in majestic chords
disturbingly like the final stanzas
of *Don Giovanni*,
and as the first flickers of fiery sunlight
chased Antares from the pink-tinged sky,
the Red Statue ambled down beneath the earth
with a last pipe-puff
and a hearty chuckle
at the *mille et tre* revolutionaries
he had sent before him
to fertilize the soil.

1989

I. Tiananmen Square

Fasting, fasting, lying foodless,
foodless in the storm-swept square,
stomachs sore and stomachs cramping,
square so crowded, stomachs void.

Millions, millions, millions hoping,
Chinese youth and workers marching,
fed up now with leaders' lying,
risking prison, risking, trying.

Gray-clad soldiers, marching, driving,
through the square of students dying,
workers now and students lying,
dead upon the tank-swept square.

II. New York

Lying in the filthy station,
home for months a trampled floor,
faces thin and faces haggard,
grime-stained mouths beseeching food.

Not this year an angry marching,
not yet here the hopeful mob,
just the pacing and the lying,
dying on the unswept floor.

A WEEK AFTER THE FIRST DESTRUCTION

Burning books sear a wound
through my repose.
Their embers will sear me
long after their last remnants are removed
from the cooling rubble
where Twin Incisors once chewed lives, expectations,
work time to nourish
profits,
where once my friends and I labored
to stymie the virus,
to combat AIDS.

Airplanes drilled cavities in these chewing Incisors,
spawning rot and destruction:
breeding war
empowering the vengeful,
evoking agendas of hatred and greed
in this "Land of Freedom" that imprisons millions,
empowers the wishes of none but the wealthy,
bullies the Earth.

A week has gone by,
a week of mourning,
a week of fear.
Today, I ride this train staring at the nothing
where Twin Incisors once glistened.
I see global wisdom impacted, in-flamed,
a terrorist victory evoking vengeful bombings
of terrorist replication
that will chew up the helpless and guiltless of Afghanistan,
spread rape and rape's infections,
rot the roots of incisive thoughts
and drill cavities in communities
by empowering Twin Viruses, HIV
and humiliation's vengeance,
to blight a chewed-up, befuddled Earth.

The Doldrums of the Years with Little Movement

Poetry has helped me get through the down-times—the weeks and months when I feared that our analysis might be wrong, that maybe the movements would not come back, that maybe the end of history had really come—except for its finale in ecological catastrophe or atomic war.

EXILE

Once, my angers terrified provosts,
my comrades filled streets
like dolphins cram tuna nets,
and my thoughts, disgusts, and anguish
vibrated to an orchestra of millions.
Now, I live as an exile,
a refugee and stranger
in the streets of my youth.
The culture has left me
to wander unsolaced through greenback ambitions,
shunned like a fart during Mozart's audition
for whispering "Marx"
as have history's yearners,
for speaking of meaning
in a slack-time of sound-bites
scrawled by accountants.

I write poems of homage or irony
about heroines and sages
unmentioned in schoolbooks,
organizers and thinkers whose failures fueled Hitler's horrors,
spurred Stalin to murder
the workers and peasants who had made a revolution,
and liquidate his comrades
who had led it,
but my fellow poets scoff at my esoterica,
my references to icepicks, Rosa, Catalonia, or Stokely
while penning paeans to camelias
or a lover's orgasmic cries.

My mind re-assures me:
It will not last . . .
the resentments of billions
will crescendo movements again.
My mind re-assures me,
but I cry still an exile,
a refugee rebel
in the land of my birth.

IN THE CATHEDRAL OF MILANO

Around me, the faithful wait impatiently to offer confession
and to burn candles for long-gone souls.
Their anguish and hopes echo those
carved in nearby statues of martyrs
as they walked to execution
or lowered loved ones off a Roman cross.

Our daily agony and faithful tithing feed this basilica of death,
rooted in centuries of fertile farmers
tilling their days under the cudgels and questions of the Inquisition
and the sharpened steel
of a nobility faithful to the ancient martyrs
and to the products of corvée labor.

Our age-old movement for freedom still cries out
like the heart of a heartless world enfleshed
in martyrs courage before
the barbarities of ancient Rome,
but like the vaulted ceilings of the cathedral
it rises only to be twisted down again
       to fetter rebellion,
       to poke holes in the condoms of safer sex,
       to demand that babies be borne by half-starved mothers,
       woman martyrs for the madmen of God.

As I walk through the aisles of Il Duomo,
I mourn for the lives crushed by its falling stones
as they built it,
for the scrimped pennies of the poor
that sustain it,
for the faith and anguish that it
grows from and in turn engenders.
It rouses feelings of faith and awe
from the sacred core of my soul,
longing for struggle,
awe at our age-old resistance,
our ability to suffer but to fight again,
and to keep our laughter and love intact
through eons painted crimson from our tortured veins,
and awe at the power of icons and altars
to transmute solidarity from struggle

into the blood and whines
of the defeated poor.

So, as I wander today through these beauteous aisles,
I long to spit on the art, take knives to the paintings
and hammer the altars and relics
like the counts, bishops and abbots
hammered rebellious peasants, craftsmen, and witches
who dared to aspire for lives of their own.

PSSSST!

Psssst! Don't look! Be still!
Glance around the room
like you're stretching your neck.
See them out there?
Some of them are even poorer
than you are.
They want . . . what you've got.
They don't deserve it.
They are an underclass.
They should worship you.
They should kiss your toes
while you rub your athlete's foot
on their tongues and hair.

Look around!
Some make what you do,
work hard, just like you.
They are good Americans.
You should work with them
to build an altar
to your betters.
But don't delay!
Each of them
wants to be
first in line
with sacrifices.
They want to beat you out
from what you deserve.

Look around again!
Some are richer than you are.
Have you licked their toes today?

Pssssst!
Don't look!
Be still!

STANDING FAST

To Harvey Swados

We stand fast.
In an era of fears,
of power grown venal,
of money, of bombers,
of bombast like cancers,
we treasure the forests,
we stand for the 'other,'
we defend love, not the power,
we speak truth to greed.

We embody defiance
as the wharfmen of Boston
scattered English pretension;
like Douglass and Tubman,
Brown, Baker and Hamer
we fight racist power,
its prisons and thefts.

If we go to the movies,
we cheer Sitting Bull's wisdom,
jeer at John Wayne
root for Viets, not Berets,
prefer Barcelona's
red-black banners of freedom
to General Patton's
flag-waving tanks.

We stand for the freedom
that brought America to birth,
for the burgeoning thoughts
that may yet save the Earth.

If We Fail

In *The Communist Manifesto*, Marx and Engels wrote "The history of all hitherto existing society is the history of class struggles. Freeman and slave, patrician and plebeian, lord and serf, guildmaster and journeyman, in a word, oppressor and oppressed, stood in constant opposition to one another, carried on an uninterrupted, now hidden, now open fight, a fight that each time ended, either in a revolutionary reconstitution of society at large, or in the common ruin of the contending classes."

I have been haunted for years by the phrase based on this, "the mutual ruin of the contending classes." What would this mean in the current context of ecological crisis and potential atomic war? What, in short, is the future like if we fail to make a successful revolution? The poems in this section speak to this issue.

A FEW YEARS DOWN THE ROAD

As she huddles, lorn, unpetted,
where she saw her people die,
a lonely cat spits last defiance
at a glaring acid sky,

but the stars stare sullen sulking
at her stricken steaming earth,
and their tears fall, fast and flaming,
through the brownish-purple sky.

There are no human hands to pet her,
No people's ears to hear
the roar of ceaseless purple gale winds
or the crashing of dead walls,
and no skin to feel the dropping,
the drop-drop-drop-drop dropping,
of the green-brown glowing acid rain.

POEM FOR COCKROACHES WHO GLOW IN THE DARK

Do not be bitter,
bereft bugs,
at the messy Earth
we've left you.
Savor the positive!
Your cancers will always be
our fault.
Your Diogenes will never lack
his lantern
lit
from within.
You will all be saints,
saints with haloes radiant and aglow.
No human hands,
no human feet,
will squash your shells,
no more
forever.

Hopes and Fears as the System Approaches Crisis

I am often surprised by the extent to which people understand that things are getting worse and worse—even though this perspective rarely gets expressed in the media except in well-scripted "don't take this too seriously" mode. Though people understand that life is getting worse and more dangerous, few see this as meaning that a major crisis is coming, or to see in this a reason for hope. I am stubborn, however, and see hope in the crisis, see the positive in the negative.

ECONOMICS OF WELFARE REFORM

As global profit rates
shrink
like the ozone above us,
politicians scurry through habitrails
to cut wages,
cut taxes,
cut costs.
Competition
is the hour's lion,
welfare recipients
a herd
of prey.
Fifty-nine months on welfare
for Maria.
No jobs in sight.
Her choices for month sixty?
One, pray for a strike,
so she can scab for freedom.
Two, starve, her only recreation
listening
to her children and neighbors
fighting
as they chew their dirt and paint scraps
amidst the strolling roaches.
Three, peddle sex for food,
go to jail,
get out,
search for her kids,
and choose again.
Four, peddle crack, go to jail, search for kids.
Five, be re-born, be a Rockefeller, Bush,
or Whitman.
Six, it's an election year.
More choices for Maria.
Vote for a Republican who hates welfare,
or vote for a Democrat who hates welfare.
Seven, form a mob.
Revolt.

WHAT'S A FELLOW GONNA DO?

Every year
it just gets harder;
harder to make an honest profit,
any profit at all.
The competition gets harder,
so our prices fall;
it takes years of red tape
to put up a goddamn building,
and years of earnings to fill it
with machinery to compete.
And all the red tape
doesn't do a damn bit of good,
the oceans and forests are dying off
anyway.
And once you make a product,
who you gonna sell it to?
They're all in jail,
or too busy working a 2nd and 3rd job
to get to the store.

Maybe I'll just close down—that'll show the bastards,
all those lazy no-good bastards
who pretend to work for me.
At least
they'll have another 60 hours a week
to shop
even if they won't have
their two hundred dollars take-home pay
to spend.
And I could retire,
find a nice sunny spot near the sea—
but not too near,
too much chemical trash to go swimming,
and the fish are too mutated
to look at,
much less eat.
A nice sunny retirement village,
for the right sort of folks,
with thick walls,
lots of security guards,
and its own private ticker tape
and community church.

THE OLD BRICK FIREHOUSE

It is 8 in the evening.
Men lie on beds
chatting
reading
sleepless, churning.

Some will rise with tomorrow's sun
to trudge to the labor exchange,
hoping to be cursed at by bosses
for a few hours or days.
Others will hang out,
shoot some dope,
deal a little,
beg,
hustle,
or steal.

On the radio,
talk show savants discuss dope fiends:
        "Kick their lazy asses
        off welfare,
        out of the shelters,
        into the streets."

In the firehouse, strung-out men stumble to the bathroom,
rub feet blistered from walking aimlessly or hauling lumber,
try to sleep.

On the news, savants worry yet again about inflation.
Too many men and women have jobs,
but the Fed will take care of *that*.

ECHO EMPTY

When my parents' parents' parents
walked towards their ships to America
long decades before I was womb-evicted
into the light of a war-rapt world,
they left families, synagogues, mezuzahs
in their Polish,   Russian,   German towns,
towns which now echo empty
of their traditions.

Now,
the ever-reverent heirs of the Nazis,
of the Roosevelt who did not bomb the trains,
and of the later Wallace
who blocked the school doors
to kids who were not White
praise families,
praise church,
praise children,
praise kitchens.

Towns echo empty
of jobs;
echo empty
of compassion;
echo empty
of solidarity.

Ovens
are heating
again.

MUSINGS OF LENIN'S GHOST, 1999

They call me evil, an evil genius,
but they were not there,
did not nightmare the tsar's prickly noose
crushing their brother's breath,
did not see strikers beaten and shot,
sabers sundering protestors' necks
beneath the seal of Father Gapon,
did not endure the years of the trenches
where young men became rotting meat
while profiteers dined on roasts
sauced by government contracts
and soldiers' parents sweated ploughshares to weapons
to slay each others' sons
and went home at midnight to rooms without coal,
without sons, without sunlight,
lives graced only by censored letters
from surviving sons
shivering in lice-filled trenches,
under the eyes of millionaires
clad in the warming woolens of generals' garb.

They call me evil because I could not forestall
their spiritual forebears' armies and blockades
that brought dispersal and death to those who built a revolution,
starved the power and imagination of those who work,
those who build,
those who grow.

They call me evil because I died too young,
because my errors were gigantic,
though smaller than Rosa Luxemburg's—
even though she saw, as I did not,
that crescendoing democracy is socialism's liver, its soul,
its magic to unlock minds,
energize caring,
propel Eisenstein and Mayakovsky to soar.

They call me evil because my so-called heirs
did unto others
as my critics advise their sons,
sought personal security and successful careers,
twisted my words,
murdered my comrades

who had been their own,
dined on the cast-out hopes and mangled hands
of workers with rooms without coal,
white-power Reds who worshipped
the givers of commands
and despised the thoughts of the workers they ruled.

They call me evil, and rejoiced at the fall
of the Communists who undid my deeds,
and they gloated as the workers of Poland
organized, rebelled, and dreamed,
drove the first mattocks into the Wall
later leveled by the workers of Berlin,
but as businessmen partied, I too rejoiced,
knowing the blues of frustration,
the rock and roll of growing hope;
and as financiers party yet again,
as their crooks take control,
their cutbacks heightening hunger,
curtailing workers' lives,
I spit upon such rejoicing,
laugh at the vainglorious bluster of these corporate fools,
fantasizers of a capitalist eternity
in which history unreels endless centuries of corporate rule,
and I await their downfall as I watch the rebirth of hope,
of thought,
of struggle

as the century ends,

as the millennium begins.

HOW COULD THEY BE SO STUPID?

"How could they be so stupid?"

This worldwide incantation is echoed,
repeated, re-echoed
in puzzle-faced grief
at species depleted
and skies without ozone,
at invasions by nations that
claim to love peace,
at the stupidity of bosses
who trample all loyalty,
at the folly of mayors
who evict men to freeze.
Again and again I hear folks wonder in pain
at acts beyond reason by powerful fools,
and I wonder myself until I remember their logic,
a logic of profit that needs greed as survival,
a system-based seeking
to compete and destroy,
to eat all your rivals
lest you be the eaten,
a logic compelled on the smart and the fools,
a logic that's heartless,
but often seems mystic,
that leaves us waddling in wondering woe,
not able to swallow the depths of the horror,
that the powerful rule us—but they're not in control,
they're driven by have-to's,
almost never by wishes,
riding a logic that drives us to ruin,
a system that's brilliant, efficient, destructive,

but need not be eternal

since it's quite in our power,

if angry in billions,

to end it forever, to tear it right

down.

KINGDOM BY THE SEA: THE BLACK BIRD OF REVOLUTION

As the walls of economic and political maneuver
inch ever inwards
like the blood-hot walls of Poe's inquisitorial pit
our rulers and their wannabe emulators
in Bonn, Tokyo, Tel Aviv, and New Delhi
sharpen the sabers that swing ever closer
to their own necks and to ours,
            the sabers on the tip of the Pendulum
                  of encroaching time.

Our rulers search frantically for a new messiah
of long-term recovery and profits restored,
            for a Keynes, a Jesus, or even an Adolph,
but as they search for their cask of amontillado,
the walls they themselves build daily
block their solutions, block their sight,
and block them from hearing the bearded raven,
that dead-and-scorned German philosopher, whisper
            "Nevermore."

The Houses of Morgan, Mitsubishi, Gates, Soros, and the Krupps
hold endless parties and soirees
as a masked Death comes to Somalia, India,
Iraq, and the Bronx,
and cholera, AIDS, and starvation
rival the sword, the Uzi and the bomb;
but their revelries come to an end
as the Death that is their system devours its own belly
as it ate the House of Usher long ago,
and the raven prognosticates,
            "Nevermore."

And as the wizards of Washington, Taipei, Beijing, Geneva and Rio de Janeiro
tootle their tunes of patriotic toil and god-fearing devotion,
of belts tightened until the belly engulfs the spine,
Annabel Lee listens her last to the talking heads.

Her laboring breath steams her dying curse
at her long-frozen radiator, at septic dope,
and at the tootlers who grasp at the sabers
at the tip of the Pendulum of encroaching time,

and the black bird of revolution caws to them,

     "Nevermore"
                 "Nevermore"
                                "Nevermore"

and to us,
        "Tomorrow."

LOT'S WIFE MEETS EURYDICE

Not looking back,
she chatted at first only
of the here and now,
the wine-stained shirts
to be stoned in the river,
the ever-repeated "do this"
"not that," "right now"
from Lot's imperious lips
(or were they Orpheus's?)
speaking his need,
never hers,
the future his path to the light,
her toiling behind,
nose clogged by his footsteps' dust,
ears straining for the whispered commands
from his wine-stained tongue
while he paces ahead,
never looking back to see
his tongue's lashing imprints,
never letting his woman think
of the wrongs ahead,
of the wrongs behind,
just demanding that she stare silent
at her master's backside,
never her own, never herstory's hopes,
neither Lot nor Orpheus daring
to face their past wrongs,
to risk an empathy that might spark hopes
of liberation,
just leaving their women to trudge tongue-tied in their dust,
behind their behinds,
so Lot's wife whispered to Eurydice's longing,
her lips burning,
passion sent,
passion received,
their hands reaching for each others' fronts,
backs,
outsides,
insides,
her message of love looking forwards,
"Next time, look back
long before."

SEARCHING

Crows fly desperate
from tree to tree,
eyes to the ground
searching for food,
searching for food
as the food,
as the food,
as the food runs out,
fighting for food
in a winter of dearth,
squabbling and battling
'til blood spots the leaves,
'til blood rushes and gushes
through acres of feathers
and butchered birds' bodies.
So bodies and feathers and blood
crowd the ground
in a land stripped of food
by a winter without
while people fly desperate
from nation to nation,
eyes to the ground
searching for oil,
searching for oil
as the oil,
as the oil,
as the oil
runs
out.

THE CENTURY WHEN HOPE DIED

This was the century when hope died,
when industry, republic, democracy vanished from imaginations
flattened by the daily pains, the daily plainness, of these dreams become
real.
This was the century of socialist hope,
of socialist revolution crushed
by the counter-revolution of bureaucrats burgeoning within,
and of social democratic hopes burst by accountancy;
the century when a black freedom movement seemed like salvation,
but sang and chanted a generation to realize that we are not saved,
that freedom to sit at a lunch counter, to vote, to ride seated at the front of a bus,
are better than not, but not butter, not guns.

This was the century when science and technology
were to eradicate hunger and disease,
a century ending amidst AIDS, bloated bellies, malaria and herpes,
where homicide became a major killer in America
and genocide and ethnic cleansing became epidemics themselves,
vectored across a century in outbreaks with ever-fewer years between,
'til we counted the "betweens" in months, not decades,
and dreaded its becoming days, this awful litany:
Armenians
Jews
Ibos
Vietnamese
Cambodians
Timorese
Hutus
Tutsi
Croats
Bosnians
Hutus and Tutsi yet again.

This was the century of hope made hopeless,
when the dreams of the seventeenth, eighteenth, and nineteenth centuries
realized themselves as nightmares,
when nations were re-born, came to adulthood,
came to murder, came to ruin.

In 1998, as in 1898, babies leave the womb to work in a world
of hunger, killing, disease.
The labors of Lenin, Luxemburg, and Lukacs
have come to naught,

but their thoughts and goals remain as our only hope of a hope,
that the working billions, the janitors, jugglers,
diggers, drivers, nannies, nurses, assemblers,
electricians, filers, fiddlers, and programmers
can dream dreams again, rebel, be defeated, and revolt again,
so the century without hope
will give way to by centuries of disbelieving children
asking "Why did they give such orders?
and why would anyone have obeyed?"

Essence: Soaring and souring and soaring again through struggle

Men make their own history, but they do not make it just as they please; they do not make it under circumstances chosen by themselves, but under circumstances directly encountered, given and transmitted from the past. The tradition of all the dead generations weighs like a nightmare on the brain of the living. And just when they seem engaged in revolutionizing themselves and things, in creating something that has never yet existed, precisely in such periods of revolutionary crisis they anxiously conjure up the spirits of the past to their service and borrow from them names, battle cries and costumes in order to present the new scene of world history in this time-honored disguise and this borrowed language. . . . .

Bourgeois revolutions, like those of the eighteenth century, storm swiftly from success to success; their dramatic effects outdo each other; men and things seem set in sparkling brilliants; ecstasy is the everyday spirit; but they are short-lived; soon they have attained their zenith, and a long crapulent depression lays hold of society before it learns soberly to assimilate the results of its storm-and-stress period. On the other hand, proletarian revolutions, like those of the nineteenth century, criticize themselves constantly, interrupt themselves continually in their own course, come back to the apparently accomplished in order to begin it afresh, deride with unmerciful thoroughness the inadequacies, weaknesses and paltrinesses of their first attempts, seem to throw down their adversary only in order that he may draw new strength from the earth and rise again, more gigantic, before them, recoil ever and anon from the indefinite prodigiousness of their own aims, until a situation has been created which makes all turning back impossible, and the conditions themselves cry out:

Hic Rhodus, his salta! (Here is Rhodes, leap here!)

(Karl Marx, *The 18th Brumaire of Louis Bonaparte.* Chapter 1.)

Struggles in our History

These poems look at struggles, including many that I have been part of and that have shaped my life, my thought, and my deepest being.

TWO-TWO-NINETEEN SIXTY

I was a high school senior
sitting on the faded pink sofa
opposite our 10-inch black-and-white TV.
Opening the Washington *Post* before heading upstairs
to homework that never went away,
my future leapt like a mischievous eel
to electrify my life.

"College students sit in.
Arrests in Greensboro."

The coffee that wasn't served,
that remained in hot pipes
                instead of steaming the mugs
of these era-busting black youth,
turned a frost-filled February into
the springtime of the century,
scalding out the sewer-years
that had been my life.

It was twelve years to the day
before my mother died
slain by the tobacco smoke and tensions
of sixty-four years in America;
and less than twenty before Ku Klux bullets
murdered my cousin's ex
in that same North Carolina town.

My childhood.
War with Japan.
War in Korea.
Earnest discussions
equating neutralism
with genocide.
Federal agents security-checking my father,
and neighbors shunning us,
when my father sought—and got—
a major promotion.
Years reading Nuclear War Comic Books,
where we thrilled at pictures
of mushroom clouds over Moscow city
and the cremation of Chelyabinsk.

As I sprouted hair on my chest and my pubis,
my soul was a constant itch,
allergic to the life around it,
but unable to see how to scratch.

My teachers droned their dedication to science, technology,
and a poetry so personal we couldn't find its persona.

My life was written in the icy pellets ringing Saturn,
to reduce the symmetries of the stars
to symbols and formulas
beautiful in their own mathematical logic,
in between scratching the unreachable itch.

But this life was not to be. I was freed
with my generation.

Our fate
and our salvation
was to walk in circles
against Jim Crow,
to walk on Woolworth's sidewalks,
to shine our butts on merry-go-rounds
that wouldn't turn
for blacks and whites together
(or any blacks at all)
while their managers offered money to hoodlums
to pound our sitting bums.

We dissolved dull decades of desolation
in years of learning to walk in loving rage,
pounding our brains to discover
the jugular of their system,
the poisons that created
our never-ending itch.

LIKE HEGEL AND MARX, I STAND FOR NEGATION

The little churches on their hillsides
resound with affirmation of their bossy God
and the rectitude of suit-and-tongue-tied congregations;

and builders of bridges radiate positivist joy
for conceiving erections like the Verrazano Narrows,
and for supervising their construction, girder by girder,
paycheck by paycheck, mortgage payment by re-done kitchen.

Their daily lives, American dreams, fade like clichés
when face to face with Negation,
with the out-of-work seamen and blistered farmers
            who caged the British within the noose-like Charles,
with sans-culottes opening minds and prisons,
            destroying the edifices of human serfdom
while the slaves of Haiti destroyed slavery itself,

with the men and women of Minneapolis, Toledo, San Francisco, and Flint
            whose strikes said "Nothing moves, nothing is built,
            no bridges erected, no workers dying in trying,
            but by our say-so,"

with the beloved communities of blacks whose aggressive suffering
            plucked Jim Crow naked
            and destroyed Southern traditions of rapine enshrined,

with the women who seized bodies and thoughts from old propriety,
            demanded that dads and communities deal with dirty diapers' joys
            negating old traditions and letting freedom in.

With Hegel and Marx, I stand for Negation.
With the strikers, beloved communities, and women revolting,
I seek the positive through destruction,
destroying the destroyers,
            building new community,
            building freedom with rage.

PATRIARCHS AREN'T THE ANSWER: AN ELEGY FOR JOHN BROWN

Green, yellow and orange foliage muted the rustles
as a few-score feet tip toed undertones
alongside the river gurgles
where the Shenandoah met the Potomac
and the babies of Harper's Ferry
dreamed of breasts
in the harvest-time dawn.

Gentle footfalls . . .
            red-leafed maples . . .
                    the BANG   BANG   BANG of muskets.

In the name of a God
who was not there,
the bearded patriarch worked miracles,
transformed a quiet harvest
and a sleeping town
into the first droplets
of a floodtime of death.

Later, as he walked to his noose
in the idyllic winter
of my native Virginia,
he may have envisioned himself
as a martyred Moses
luring slave-owning Pharaohs
into a red sea of their own blood.

But his fantasies were foredoomed
by his own inner being,
his own patriarch self,
as the millions of slaves--
who had no part in the planning--
did not yet rally to the autumn hills
or seize the streets of Harper's Ferry.

These slaves acted only later,
writing words far brighter than the Biblical graffiti
on Babylon's burning walls:

"Liberation comes from the oppressed,
from our own thoughts,
our own actions,
our own fatal mistakes,
at our own chosen time."

And so the Union armies struggled from defeat
to defeat
to defeat
until the slaves sabotaged the making
and hauling
of Confederate arms and foods of war,
or walked off to freedom,
leaving their owners to hoe,
and until the slaves-made-free forced Lincoln to arm them
(though, fatally, to command them too).
Their bodies and minds swelled the faltering Union forces with new troops,
new dedication,
new victory,

but a victory that was never theirs,
led by a rail-splitting president
whose contracts enriched and empowered rail-laying capital,
built a nation dedicated to industrial profits
as its new Moses and prophets,
disarm the blacks for slave-cropping lifetimes,
dis-voice them into de-mobilized prey.

RIDING WITH MARTIN

We rode the ride alongside Martin,
some faster, some slower,
some taking sideroads to who-knew-where,
but all of us learning,
learning,
learning,
learning nonviolence,
learning mass action,
learning that blessed communities
live lives sundered by race, class, and sex.
We learned the limits of liberalism,
the limits of guilt,
when liberals silenced the voice of our truth,
demanded we stop sit-ins and marches lest votes be lost
for liberal politicians.
We learned the evils of liberalism
when liberals sent bombs to kill peasants
in Nam and Dominica,
drafted the young from blessed communities
to creep through jungles
as prey for mosquitoes
and enemies of all.

And as we rode with King
so we learned
as did he
about power,
about the power of wealth,
the power of police, and the power of armies.
Though divided now by race and gender,
and riven by class,
we all faced the truth
that our strength was too feeble.
We learned the limits of truth,
the limits of our power,
of communities beneath
the power of money,
of racist money as capital,
and of racist police
backed up by an army.

We faced the question, "What next?"
of who should do what with whom
for what ends
        that a nation of white profits,
        for white profits,
        and by white profits
could be vanished from Earth.

And as we rode with Martin
as a new-born melánge of movements,
we learned together,
argued together,
sought new pathways together
though we lived well apart...

and Martin proclaimed a beginning,
his beginning,
"to question the capitalist economy,"
to see racism, exploitation, and war,
as one.*

After Martin fell
beneath the guns of our enemies,
his learning stopped,
his ideas and his memory
seized, twisted, transformed
by the liberals he had grown far apart from.

Now, his revolutionary children
face condemnation
in the name of a Martin
whose future choices,
whose future learning,
remain
forever

unknown.

*SCLC Presidential Address, 1967

...THEREFORE, I AM

After the malaise
of younger teenage years
in the hate-filled, fearful fifties,
sit-ins, picket lines,
and years of massive demos
taught me thought,
organizing,
the analytics and dialectics
of human freedom,
taught me that Descartes' rigid logic
graphed not the truth
of human life, human striving.

Emergence was through sit-ins,
Being through demos,
Essence through seeking ever more change,
seeking our power, free and transcendent.

We struggle,
therefore, I am.

WHEN I WAS 32

When I was 32, and the new guy in town,
two months on the job,
knowing very few,
teaching on a campus
32 miles from home,
driving the Garden State
with the morning sun
on my right,
driving home under stars as the nights grew colder,
promising snow-days
— they called a strike.

Monday, 5 a.m.
Creep from home,
drive the empty Parkway north,
Route 3 west then down Valley Road,
park across the street
so I won't have to scab the line
to go home.
Wait alone on the side of the road
holding a sign, unsure
whether I'll ever work again
at a paying job.
But then they came, signs in hands,
one here, two there, 'til dozens
then scores
of signs danced in the pre-Thanksgiving air,
"On strike, shut it down."
Eight days on the line,
meeting new friends,
cops hot and cold
sometimes friendly,
but always supporting the employer's rights
while the traffic backed up for a mile
and students and faculty learned
three years' lessons every day.
On strike!
Living free!
Walking together,
toeing our line,
not the bosses'.

DIANA'S DREAMS

It is hard to intuit
the thoughts of a younger Diana,
the student Diana
who talked Marx and revolution
as friends were disappeared,
their bodies tortured,
then disposed.

What must her fears have been?
Her nightly dreams?
Her waking dreads?
Her hatreds?
I have never dared to ask.

When I visit, we talk of everything
other:
Our joy sipping Malbec,
our families and friends,
our efforts to stop the spread of AIDS,
my years in the Movements
when the USA stirred,
even her politics
in the days of dictatorship,
or the slow decay of civility
in Buenos Aires today,
the encroaching barbarism
in the USA,
and the struggles against them—
anemic and timid
in my homeland of insecurity,
powerful and free in the land
where her friends once screamed
their final pain—

but we never discuss
our fears when we were young,
when friends were stabbed
and friends were beaten,

when then we dreamed.

GENERATION

I am a member of a tired generation
that spent ten years walking
walking walking
when not sitting in
and then fifteen more years
in endless meetings about
how to have company when
we walk some more.

We opened our own eyes with
auto-jacks of love and toil
only to have our treasured understandings
be seen as "of course." But
our friends spent years on each passé
fact and connection
and sometimes we learned them only
as some of us died.

Was it really so hopeless as
the young ones now say?
Were we tilting with lances of gossamer
at raging winds of unconcern and
furnaces of power?
Or does there lie ahead
a tap root of anger
at lost possibilities
and rage at a war-threatened Earth
that can lift us as one
redeemer
to take back our world?

Note: This was my first poem to be published.

OUR SIGN SAYS "HONK IF YOU HATE WAR"

Some few praise death
as they drive past us,
yell "Get a job"
to John who, in his '70s, still professes to students
and to me, 62, and a slave to AIDS research.
Some put their thumbs down
and call us losers.
Others put their middle fingers up
and drive smugly past
like teenagers just learning
driving and smut.
We hold our signs
that call for an end to war,
wave our friendship to all the passing cars,
accept with smiles and thumbs up
the airhorn salutes of passing truckers,
the beeps of new cars, old cars,
fancy cars, plain cars,
buses, and mail vans
and the verbal greetings of pedestrians
who say "honk, honk."
Many thank us.
Few deride.

HEROES

The point is
Everyone
was a hero,
Everybody who acted,
who put their body
on the line.
Each of us knew the risks,
had heard the stories
of gunshots, beatings,
Congressional committees,
shattered careers,
jailhouse tortures.
But each of us acted,
thought . . . inspired,
each was a hero,
everyone who dared.
Sure, the press covered
Martin, Stokely,
Gloria and Cesar,
and occasionally even Fannie Lou,
and these folks sure were
heroes,
but so were Amy & Lois & Tom
who picketed Glen Echo with me
in the summer of '60,
and Eric and Laurie and Tom
who shared some jail time
after we demo'd a draft board,
the first time ever, in sixty-five,
and so were millions of others
no one ever hears of anymore
because the press and the politicians
and the employers
just don't want us to know
we can all be heroes—
just pick up a sign
and march or vigil,
sit in, or strike,
and take away their power
so our time and bodies
can be
free.

AIDS Struggles

I have been very involved in AIDS struggles as a result of—but not a part of—my job.

REDISCOVERY

After 15 years of learning labor,
learning strikes,
being scoffed at by academics
who saw class as passé
while benefiting mightily
for such views,
I retreated into AIDS,
researching an epidemic of savage viruses and of vicious hate.
I learned odds ratios, risk factors,
networks, and the exchange of syringes,
met the bottom-crawlers abandoned beneath
the class system, sneered at as junkies
by their fellow poor,
by homeless alcoholics,
women on welfare,
the street-wanderers battered by time,
who console their lives by despising
those who shoot drugs,

and I rediscovered resistance amongst the shooters,
amongst syringistas who refused to die,
who rejected the hatred and rejected the labels
and saw through their evil;
and I rediscovered the horror of class society
in their pain,
rediscovered its solution in their struggles,
their clarity of thought,
and the ever-repeated evidence
that those the system would destroy

rebel.

NEEDLE EXCHANGE DEMO, TRENTON, NEW JERSEY, STATEHOUSE, JANUARY 12, 1999

"You killed my father,"
the young woman screamed
as the crowd applauded her thought, her fury, her truth,
just as they cheered the ex-user
who condemned New Jersey's government
for denying needles,
urging users to seek treatment
while starving treatment of funds,
and chanted to their governor,
"Christy Whitman, you can't hide,
we charge you
with genocide,"

while gray-uniformed cops guarded the doors
from the anger of hundreds
protesting state-sanctioned death
from AIDS, the modern plague.

But, elsewhere in New Jersey,
it was business as usual:
two blocks away,
the governor proposed tax rebates for homeowners
to raving Republicans and Democrats
with welfare and drug treatment budgets as collateral
while Aetna bought up health-care-for-profit,
ECCS and other faceless companies laid off workers,
and the madness and fears of holding a job
grew more frenetic
everywhere.

Off-stage, cops hunted junkies and the exchangers of needles.
wile viruses thrived like the owners of corporations,
and politicians grinned before cameras
in this State denying needles,
bullish on death.

They
have the
power.

For now.

CONFERENCES

> Dedicated to the attendees of the 1995
> North American Syringe Exchange Convention

What I see is love around me
love in action, love in deeds
love among the hundreds of trench-fighters
impatient doers who keep at it,
preventing new infections
while suffering sneers
every day
every week
every year
love in action
love in deeds
love, sometimes twisted
into spiteful words
          resentment
          envy
          greed
          aspiration for fame,
          desire for respect,
          twisting love
          into griping distrust.

Sometimes,
what looks like conflict
is really love,
when two or more people face off
across the faces
of a silent meeting room
to show each the other
why the other is wrong,
why the mistakes can cost hundreds
of new infections.
These words may be bitter
but they embody love
and after the session
these battlers go out for a chat
or to plan new ways
to battle the hated virus
and the powers that support it.

Beneath the honest conflicts
beneath the painful shyness
the envy
resentment
backbiting
and occasional spite
what I see is love around me
total support among the bickerers
when the shit hits the plan
when the friends of the virus
or the care-less careerists
besiege one of the battlers
total support
love in action
love in deeds
love among the trench-fighters
love—
and we need it.

HOLY NASEC, APRIL 28, 2001

As the band played on,
and
needle exchangers danced
a spirit of holiness pervaded our tables
and the smiles of the chatterers,
the maturity of a movement grown holy
through the pains of our errors,
through losing friends to the virus,
some deaths due to our errors,
some caused by our love,
but many prevented,

many prevented,

more and more, many prevented,
our errors transcended
through arguments extended
to respect and deep friendship;
so we chat and we party,
a roomful of doers,
of queers, straights, and junkies,
a roomful of saints transcendent and holy,
purveyors of points despite the fangs of the power,
purveyors of needles through decades of plagues.

(Note: NASEC is the North American Syringe Exchange Convention)

Future Struggles—We Hope

I have long believed that the survival of the human race—and many other species—requires the revolutionary abolition of the capitalist system and its replacement by a system that is not compelled to expand to the point of extinction. For several decades, then, I have shivered at the global political success of neoliberal defenders of this system, and marveled at their ability to squeeze and attack almost everybody and yet turn the resulting fear and guilt into support for more of the same.

Of course, every time rebellion has shown its head, I hoped and hoped that it would break into a liberatory movement of billions.

These poems are about the fire next time.

VISIONS OF NOW, TOMORROW, AND BEYOND

Now
Syringe tops shine orange by the crack vials
on the sparkling snow of Brooklyn.
Penn Station, refurbished, is clear of beggars,
who shiver in the great outdoors
while commuters line up to buy baked goodies
as they wait for their trains.
A commuter train engineer,
on a 14½ hour stint of duty,
envisions another train as a bed to hop into;
it is the last fantasy of two engineers
and a commuter,
but the other train lines do business as usual.
A few late-to-the-ball geese had gamboled their way southwards
through carcinogenic frozen air.
Their honking should have warned the engineer,
but he was too tired to hear it.
The next flight of geese
takes snapshots of the wreckage.

Thirty thousand janitors shiver in the cold
while cops stand around making jokes
about homeless ex-janitors
and protect scabs
in the name of freedom and the American Way.
In Short Hills and the Upper East Side,
designer clothing and post-modern art
sell at record prices
to the discerning few.

Echoing laughter
by the Bourbon Kings
and Tyrannosaurus Rex.

Tomorrow
The crumbling of an abandoned
snakeskin.

Streets
fill with strikers.
Scabs
run for their lives
as cops

hand their guns and billy clubs to the rioters.
People walk calmly through the aisles of FAO Schwartz
taking toys for their toddlers
and for the new playgrounds they will build.
Nobody is at the cash registers,
and the sun shines gaily.
The hot topic that everyone is talking about
is how to structure the agendas of meetings
so everyone gets an equal voice
and creativity is encouraged instead of stifled.

Beyond
Dust blows through the shattered windows
of a long-outdated bank.
Corn pushes its silken ears
through the five-sided ruins
that once were a Pentagon.
Children laugh in disbelief
at parents' tales of evictions,
layoffs
scabs
and the giving of orders.

LOAFERS

As the earth slowly sheds its green-leaf hair,
the iron law of competition compels
a Congress of driven hyenas
to enact a postmodern
Law of the Wild:
Sit, smile, and be eaten.

The media pump old wine
for new battles:
Cops are angelic avengers
schools and welfare are costs
health is a drain on taxpayers' wallets.
Prisons and security technology are growth stocks.

If you are poor,
it's your own fault.
Go to jail, or get a job.
Start your own brokerage firm.
Welfare is out.
Prisons are in.
Be stylish—go to prison;
wear their baggy overalls
to hide your protruding bones.

When the squalling of hungry children
drives you to steal a loaf of bread
think of Jean Valjean.
One loaf equals five years.
Two loaves equal ten.
Three loaves and you're out.
For life,
you recidivist loafer, you.
While you are locked up waiting a year for your trial,
we will sell your children;
or maybe put them to work
sweeping syringes from the floors
of shooting galleries.
While you are in jail,
we will not let you watch Les Miserables,
nor even read the book.
It was written by a foreigner.

If you are ever released,

we will introduce you to Inspector Javert,
to hundreds of Inspector Javerts.
All of them will be assigned
to catch you if you steal more bread,
to tell potential employers you have a record,
and to plant crumbs in your pocket.

So, as the earth doffs its ozone layer
in respect for free enterprise,
let us think again of Les Miserables,
of Jean Valjean,
and all the Jeanette Valjeans
who truly deserve to drive their children to school
in the Cadillacs of media fantasy,
but who count each grain of rice and divide every bean
into slivers for their children,
and who crouch behind rusty dumpsters in fear of rape
when squad cars drive by.
Let us work for the end of this system
that pits all against all,
leaves all but a few at the mercy
of the few
who give jobs,
that values prisons over schools,
cops over the hungry,
the chain gang over the safety net,
the bottom line over love, leisure, and the lives of those on the bottom.
Let us remember Jean Valjean,
let us remember 1832, 1848, and 1871,
let us invent a new
revolution.

A Turnpike Utopia

Ducks fill the Turnpike,
a-waddle, in rows,
a swelling rebellion
en marche to D.C.

Row after row
of web-footed marchers
drop trails of fresh guano
across twelve asphalt lanes.

Ducks fill the Roy Rogers,
the Big Boys and Hardees,
they order their dinners,
demand them "to go."

They soar from lake acids to
land on the on-ramps,
they crowd up the off-ramps,
feet slimy with goo;

they waddle the highway
by bird-shrouded autos,
they honk up at the drivers
indignant with rage.

The windshields are covered
with web-footed quackers,
and tires slide spinning
through guano and oil.

Their mouths pointing skywards
ducks bill-board their protest—
          they quack forth their horror
          at ponds full of benzene,
          they weep for their rivers
          all covered with scum.

The swans and the egrets
form allied contingents,
their feathers reflecting
a white like the sun's.

The pigeons await them
on Washington's statues,
the robins bomb guano
on snarled limos below.

The geese seize the White House,
as ducks fill the Senate;
their quackery fills
the Capitol's dome.

Their guano makes fertile
the halls and the rostra,
replacing the bullshit
where money once reigned.

IMAGINE #2

Imagine a 4-year old riding her tricycle
through her yard of bee-symphonied dandelions
while parents and friends nibble drumsticks
and her older sister sonatas Mozart to dandelioned bees
on her birthday-gift violin.

Imagine as the mortgage cracks,
the father splits, the drumsticks transmute
into borrowed potatoes,
the violin to a pawnshop chit,
the yard to a glass-littered pothole,
the friends to see-ya-sometime,
the mom to worn-through bluejeans
with eyes of jaundice
instead of dandelions.

Imagine alcohol, imagine beatings,
imagine a hundred million 4-year olds
with bellies bloated as a gasbag-politician's words,
imagine a system bloated with Tahitian vacations
and Javanese junkets
at the top.

Imagine four billion clenched fists,
four billion angry eyes aglow with ideas instead of jaundice,
imagine six billion minds creating thoughts beyond dandelions, beyond drum-
sticks,
imagine bodies and minds taking power and creating a world
where four-year-olds can live.

Notion: Making the World Anew

For as soon as the distribution of labour comes into being, each man has a particular, exclusive sphere of activity, which is forced upon him and from which he cannot escape. He is a hunter, a fisherman, a herdsman, or a critical critic, and must remain so if he does not want to lose his means of livelihood; while in communist society, where nobody has one exclusive sphere of activity but each can become accomplished in any branch he wishes, society regulates the general production and thus makes it possible for me to do one thing today and another tomorrow, to hunt in the morning, fish in the afternoon, rear cattle in the evening, criticise after dinner, just as I have a mind, without ever becoming hunter, fisherman, herdsman or critic.

Karl Marx & Friedrich Engels, *The German Ideology*

". . . not a static Communist utopia but an evolving human community."

Adrienne Rich, *Arts of the Possible*, p. 86 (in chapter on "Raya Dunayevskaya's Marx")

AFTER, ON THE WAY TO THEREAFTER

After the Heartbreak House of fighting,
and after the fire next time,
after the parties, the toasting and cheering
when none will bewail
that capitalism has been erased,
we will build our global city
like a flower from the ashes
with its roots suckled and fed and watered
by the local and daily and real.
One petal will be the friendships of work time,
another our neighbors, as we talk and we share.
Those who sew diapers, those who pin them and change them,
will share with the planners, will help shape the towers,
the basement foundations
and the neighborly labor of digging,
of digging and building our city anew.

And so, in the morning, I may scrape out a waste dump,
figuring out how with my pals on the job.
In my 2 p.m. gig, I may write a paper on AIDS,
or hug and console
a stranger or friend.
My evening, perhaps, put our heads in the oven
as we clean a community stove,
or I may weave a poem, or rest overlong,
or whatever seems needed and fun
as we build our embraceable
new global city
from the petals and rootings of dreams.

AUGUST OUTAGE

Computers
light bulbs
elevators
subways
the blowers of cooling air
stand suddenly useless,
silent, gone.
Voices can now be heard.
Stairwells utter
descending feet.
Sweating bodies herd streets
swap tales and rumors of buses
exhausted.
Those with ideas or water bottles
share.

In my five hours wandering without electrons
on the midtown streets of Manhattan,
in the ghetto core of Plainfield, NJ,
and throughout the long bus-sit between,
I hear no hostility,
share confusion, water, and thoughts
with many strangers,
make many friends
of the moment,

of this moment when solidarity flowers,
this moment nested between years
of shoving, pressure,
talons,
fangs.

DEREGULATION

Squirming bodies
like kittens in a bag
bump jostle squeeze
waiting . . . waiting . . . . waiting
hoping to get on the plane.

Weak-voiced airline rep
mutters corporate reassurances.
Some yell, some scoff,
no one believes.
Mood . . . ? turning ugly.

Overbooking. Some won't get on.

Shouting at each other, jostling,
squeezing forward,
hour after hour after hour.
A few tell jokes,
talk our humanity,
but no one says good
about the airline.

Three hours pass.
We have blossomed
friendships
jokes
smiles
in a miasma of 85-degree air
that moves no more than
the crowd
or the airplane
which may be
approaching the gates--
or may not (who knows?)
No jostling,
no vying pushing shoving,
just caring for kids
coping
helping.

MARXMAS FOR MUZAK

I'm a Karlo-Groucho Marxist,
and it's nearing Christmas Day,
the buildings carol Muzak
of a Holy Babe and Sleigh.

Jews wear muffs and mumbles,
Moslems hide in fear,
but we Marxists bear glad tidings
of a sometime, hoped-for, year:

"Every day will glitter friendship,
time to chat at work and home,
debts and hunger will be unknown myths,
as will nagging unpaid loans.

When we have ended corporate rule,
each will have an equal say,
we'll have time to learn in pleasure
and our work will feel like play.

Then Christmas Now and Christmas Next
will be careless days of cheer,
the woes of then-gone Christmas Past
just children's storied fears."

SECOND NEGATION: NOTES ON THE DAY AFTER THE REVOLUTION

As crowds party loudly on glass-glittered sidewalks
and dodge around potholes while promenading the Bowery,
and offices and sweatshops echo crescendos
as workers debate how
they should now run them,
and what wonders to build
with their minds and their hands.,
I wander alone, alone among revelers,
with notebook in hand while I mutter and scribble,
jotting elation and jotting my fear.

The TVs in the windows replay it,
replay the Weeks of the Wonders --
how, after the years of the cynics,
when words of revolution led only to mutters of "not in my lifetime,"
we began having strikes again in New York and in Jersey;
and how, a couple of weeks ago, a boss in a tall box near the river
said "girl"
to one of the secretaries --
and everybody -- mailroom clerks, secretaries, truck drivers, even analysts --
walked out,
but then walked back in again
and sent the bosses home.
        Then, of course, the mayor called the cops,
        the governor called the National Guard,
        and the President the Army --
but everybody had been there,
everyone had been called "girl" or "boy" or "kike" or "Polack" or maybe
"rookie" or "grunt" --
so our rulers called the cops,
        and they called the Marines,
            and they called and they called and they called and they called,
but workers and neighbors argued with cops, joked with the Guard,
sang solidarity with the soldiers,
        and the now-rebel workers and soldiers beat up the few
        who would not see reason,
        and they all went home --
                or joined the crowd.
So the American peoples said "Enough! It's all over!"
and workers stopped working
        and crowds seduced armies
           and only 18 died in all the Americas
and a few score more died, across the green globe.

By the flickering light of the Tubes in the windows,
I wander through littered streets
once built by the defunct civilization
that brought us Agent Orange, pet stones, and AIDS for the millions,
and I rejoice as I dread
                    and I dread as I rejoice.

And as I wander, I wonder:
        "What the hell do we do next?"

I mean, after the subtle pleasures --
        like making the bosses work 4 or 5 months doing some of the *real fun*
        jobs,
        like repairing the tops of blast furnaces
        or changing the linens in the ICUs;
        and letting the ex-cops sleep on the park benches
        and on the floor of the bus station,
        so we can cheerily poke them awake,
        crying, "Time to move on now," with a big grin and a big stick.

I mean,
        what the hell do we do next?

Spectres hover over my shoulder:
        the thousands of Communards gunned down by Reaction,
        Rosa and Karl murdered by the goon squads of social democracy,
        the telephone exchange in Barcelona —
        where Uncle Joe "reached out and gouged someone,"
        and throttled the soul of a revolution —
dance with dreams of ice picks in my fear-torn, grinning head.

I mean,
        what the hell do we do next?

Sure, the market's got to go, but what do we replace it with?

How will we get the food grown
        and have all the candy, bread, and roses we need
        for the photo-journalists
        and our children?

How will we live our meanings, and not just numbers?

How do we unleash the sleeping poetry? the smothered power to create that
        waits like crabgrass
        in the brains and hands of everyone,
even in the slit-eyed grimaces of the nay-sayers
who wear red tape
instead of suspenders?

Like crabgrass, these five billion poets will shoot forth trillions of pages
        filled with tripe and doggerel
        which someone – maybe even me -- will have to read,
        pages filled with crackpot ideas redolent of disaster,
but salvation scattered throughout -- if we can find it.

So here I wander,
thinking of these Galileos and Miltons we need to create our new world,
and the humongous arguments that will fill our ears
as they shout forth their insights against each other,
and I ponder the epic mistakes our revolutionary democracy
is undoubtedly making
even as I rove, wander and scribble
through the rubble, the wonders, and the shoving salvation
as crabgrass pushes aside the arid asphalt of Madison Avenue
to seek its sun
and in so doing pushes the fears from my heart
(but not from my next-day mind)
and I walk grinning into the nearest party
to join the celebration
and raise glass after glass in toasts of global unison
with friends in Santos and Granada, Bangkok and Kampala,
Melbourne, Tacoma, Portland, and Detroit.

Appendices

Appendix 1: Review of *Philosophy and Revolution*, by Raya Dunayevskaya

Philosophy and Revolution: From Hegel to Sartre, and from Marx to Mao, by Raya Dunayevskaya. Lanham, MD: Lexington Books, 2003. xliv + 377 pp. ISBN: 0-7391-0559-0.
Published in *Contemporary Sociology* 34;1(2005):77-78, .

Raya Dunayevskaya, was a political activist and self-taught Hegel and Marx scholar. She was one of the remarkable generation of socialist intellectuals who grew up with the Russian Revolution but who in or around the 1930s became involved with Trotskyist politics only to split from Trotskyism when they came to see that Russia had become an exploitation-driven class society that was Other to the workers' movement and to socialism. Political activists and thinkers like Tony Cliff, Hal Draper and CLR James were among her contemporaries, as were many who became leading sociologists and social philosophers such as Daniel Bell, Lewis Coser, Sidney Hook, and Philip Selznick.

All of these thinkers and doers focused in different degrees on two major questions:

1.   How do workers' movements become turned around and become exploiters (Russia) or bureaucratized fetters upon the workers (the CIO leadership)?

2.   How can the socialist movement "get it right" next time? Or, in Dunayevskaya's Marxist Humanist approach, based firmly on Hegel, how can the first negation (of capitalism) through a revolution by workers and what she called "new passions and new forces" (like the Black movement, anti-Vietnam War youth, and women) generate a second negation that leads to the making of a new world?

Dunayevskaya's answers to these questions in this book (which was first published in 1973; the present edition includes useful Forewords by Louis Dupré and Erich Fromm) are evocative and profound. They are sometimes hard to fathom for those of us who were trained as sociologists and (at least in my case) exposed to no Hegel and almost no Marx as part of our graduate or undergraduate training. The book has a long chapter on Hegel which presents his work through the lens of Dunayevskaya's Marxism; a chapter on Marx which interprets his thought from the perspective of his use of the Hegelian dialectic; and a chapter on Lenin and, as Dunayevskaya--and more recently, Anderson (1995)— put it, his "shock of recognition" when he partially reorganized his thinking and politics upon reading Hegel's two books on *Logic* (1975, 1989) after what he saw as the Social Democracy's switching to the capitalist side at the outbreak of World War I. She also has chapters on Trotsky, Mao, Sartre, the African movements that ended colonial rule, the East European revolts against what she saw as state capitalism, and the "new passions and new forces."

Of great interest to readers concerned with issues of identity and subjectivity, Dunayevskaya shows the centrality of these issues to Hegelian and Marxist thought. As she sees it, the subjectivity of workers, Blacks, women, students and others is central to the emergence of the forces that can negate capitalism, and are even more central to the processes of re-making the world into a form where humans can be free, creative and happy. Such subjectivity is also a central methodological category. Dunayevskaya discusses (see particularly pp. 68 – 76) the ways in which workers' struggles, including the struggles of British workers against American slavery during the Civil War and the struggle of the slaves in the American South during this same conflict, shaped the structure and ideas of Marx's *Capital*. She concretizes this as a methodological principle for social research—that the understandings developed by grassroots struggles of all kinds provide a crucial insight into society and, even more, she sees the emergence of the working class and other struggling groups as the source of new forms of philosophy and reason. This insight goes far beyond those of participatory action research, and in some ways even beyond those of Paulo Freire (1973). For those of us who lived through the 1960s and saw (and took part in) the renewal of sociology, economics, political science, philosophy and other fields by the movements of that period, her analysis reads true.

In closing, I want to recommend this book in spite of the fact that it is a hard read. Together with Dunayevskaya's other work—and particularly *Marxism and Freedom* (1958) and *The Power of Negativity* (2002)—her work has led me to a serious engagement with Hegel. This has proved invaluable to me in thinking about topics as disparate as:

(a)   The relationship of the human immunodeficiency virus (HIV) to the immune system; and

(b)   The insight into human liberation that can be gained if we do not think of periods after workers' revolutions in terms of utopian models of reconstruction; but rather view them as periods of problems and opportunities that create contradictions and thus struggles that can lead to new modes of freedom, human solidarity, and both individual and collective creativity (Friedman 2004).

References

Anderson, Kevin. 1995. *Lenin, Hegel, and Western Marxism*. Chicago: University of Illinois Press.

Dunayevskaya, Raya. 1958. *Marxism and Freedom*. New York: Bookman.

Dunayevskaya, Raya. 1973. *Philosophy and Revolution*. New York: Dell.

Dunayevskaya, Raya. 2002. *The Power of Negativity*. New York: Lexington.

Freire, Paulo. 1973. *Pedagogy of the Oppressed*. New York: Seabury Press.

Friedman, Samuel R. 2004. Outside the Dialectic. 2004. *Historical Materialism* 12;2.

Hegel, GWF. 1975. *Hegel's Logic*. Translated by William Wallace. New York: Oxford University Press.

Hegel. 1989. *Hegel's Science of Logic*. (trans. AV Miller). Atlantic Highlands: Humanities Press International.

Appendix 2: Notes on the Practical Idea and the Russian Revolution: A letter of commentary on *Lenin, Hegel, and Western Marxism*

Note: An edited form of this article was published by *News and Letters*

> *Every act of becoming conscious*
> *(it says here in this book)*
> *is an unnatural act.*
> Adrienne Rich, *Diving into the Wreck.*
> New York: Norton, 1973: p. 31.

Kevin Anderson's recent *Lenin, Hegel, and Western Marxism* (Chicago: University of Illinois Press, 1995) focuses on an analysis of Lenin's reading of Hegel after the beginning of World War I; the uses he made of his insights into Hegel; and the ways Lenin's reading of Hegel did and did not influence Western Marxism. Here, I want to pick up on a few of my disagreements with Anderson's argument and to see where they lead in terms of political implications.

Let me start by saying that Anderson's book is terrific. Unlike many analyses of Hegel and Marxism, it is comprehensible. Beyond that, it lays out an analysis that is coherent, sensible, and useful. Furthermore, even where it seems to me to be wrong, its clarity and strength make it possible to see how an understanding of these mistakes or omissions can be corrected and the political implications of this.

One of the major mistakes Anderson makes is one where he has good company, including both Lenin and Dunayevskaya. Anderson sees Lenin as having been led by his reading of Hegel to an analysis of imperialism that sees the working class as containing a workers' aristocracy that is the root of reformism. As capitalism moves into its monopoly face, then, new forms of subjectivity, including both nationalist movements and the socialism of the lower sections of the working class, become the new opposition and, in the Russian Empire at least, the new and successful revolutionary subject. Anderson, following Dunayevskaya, sees this as a brilliant example of how Marxists who understand Hegel can analyze the dialectics of capitalism and act to end this hideous system.

Anderson, however, then builds on this analysis of Lenin's in ways that lead him to misunderstand some of what Lenin says and then to move backwards from Lenin rather than ahead in one crucial area of thought. On p. 143, Anderson fails to *theorize* the fact that Lenin, in writing about "a whole series of democratic and revolutionary movements, including the national liberation movement, in the undeveloped, backward and oppressed nations" is assuming *as obvious* that these movements include socialist workers' movements as well as nationalist movements. Examples of such movements that Lenin discussed at that time included the workers' movements in Poland and Ireland; and the course of the Chinese revolution of the 1920s made it obvious that the workers' movements were a critical component of what he was talking about. By p. 249,

Anderson is emphasizing these "new forms of subjectivity" to the point that he criticizes Western Marxism as emphasizing philosophy and culture to the point that they become "cut off from living social movements in the industrialized countries and the Third World, movements of people of color, youth, and women." His critiques of much of Western Marxism as cut off from movements is indeed, and tragically, true—but it is also very upsetting that he here does not theorize the fact that they are *even more cut off from the movements of the working class*. This is not, of course, to deny that, in practice, Anderson and, indeed, Dunayevskaya and *News and Letters* do engage in working class politics. It is, however, to suggest that the primary advocates for a Marxism that builds on Hegel should not discount the major lesson that Marx learned in his youth: That it is the working class, and its subjective movement—including, to be sure, its dialectical interrelationships with the "new social movements" which embrace both workers and non-workers—that are the key to human liberation.)

Unfortunately for their arguments, Lenin, Dunayevskaya, and Anderson are historically wrong about the theory of the labor aristocracy. I have presented this argument in some detail in prior articles (Friedman, 1983; 1986), so I will not belabor it here. In brief, the movements throughout Europe (and the United States) at the end of World War I involved *both* the "labor aristocracy" and workers from lower strata, and if anything it was the "aristocratic" workers who led in the formation of soviets in Russia, the radicalization of Glasgow, Berlin, Paris, and Turin; the railroad and building trades radicalization in France; and the Seattle general strike (Cole 1958: Ch. 13; Cronin 1980; Dewar 1976; Fischer 1948; Hinton & Hyman 1975; Kendall 1969; Lorwin 1954; Milton 1973; Moore 1978, particularly 287-88; Nettl 1969; Pelling 1958; Sirianni 1983; Spriano 1964; Williams 1973.) Furthermore, near-revolutionary episodes in France (1968), Italy (1969-70), Portugal (1975), Hungary (1956), Poland (early 1980s), and the workers' movements in Argentina, Brazil and Chile, have all also followed the pattern of having "aristocrats" as an important, and in some cases primary, part of the radicalization.

One question that we need to consider, then, is what are the political and philosophical implications if Anderson, Dunayevskaya, and Lenin were wrong on this issue. Does it mean that the entire analysis of imperialism was wrong? that Lenin's analysis of imperialist economism (still one of the best theoretical refutations of those who oppose affirmative action and other programs against racism) was wrong? that the dialectical analyses coming out of their reading of Hegel were wrong? I suggest, instead, that their error was in not taking the implications of Hegel far enough—that is, that they retreated to a "vulgar materialist" analysis in seeing the contradictions within the working class as primarily based on *economic* divisions among workers rather than being *subjective* (i.e., political). Lenin, to his credit, nonetheless acted in practice in full recognition of the primacy of the political divisions among workers, and this enabled him to develop the politics of 1917.

Let us talk now about another aspect of Anderson's book (which will be unified with the above analysis below). Perhaps the core of my argument here flows from asking myself "What was Lenin thinking about when he wrote about the Practical Idea?" Lenin writes (*CW* 38: 216) that "What is necessary is the *union of cognition* and *practice*;" and Anderson (p. 81) goes on to note that Lenin's thought here involves "the development of self-conscious subjectivity aware of its own actuality." Anderson then notes (p. 82) that Lenin omits to write down some of Hegel's key ideas, including "But what is still lacking in the practical Idea is the moment of consciousness proper itself, namely, that the moment of actuality in the Notion should have attained on its own account the determination of *external being*. Another way of regarding this defect is that the *practical* Idea still lacks the moment of the *theoretical* Idea" (Hegel 1989: 821). There is somewhat of an insufficiency in Anderson's discussion of this point, however. He does not seriously discuss who or what it is that Lenin sees as being subjective. In particular, is it the working class as a whole? the working class as a divided, dialectical process? the party? or what?

I suggest that, for Lenin, the Practical Idea meant the *party*—the party, it is true, in dialectic with the working class, and the party as a dialectically-changing formation, but nevertheless the party. Here, Anderson and Dunayevskaya would then probably say that the problem is for the working class to "get philosophy"— that is, that it "lacks the moment of the *theoretical* Idea." Furthermore, they would correctly emphasize that "getting philosophy" requires philosophical knowledge, creativity, discussion, and hard work on the part of organized revolutionaries. My analysis of Lenin, however, is that he focused on the need for a *party*, and for that party to have the politics it needed, for his whole life (while, as Dunayevskaya and Anderson have pointed out, downplaying the role of philosohical knowledge and discussion in the party and the class). Farber (1990) offers some useful insight here. His book showed that Lenin's party (and Lenin, although perhaps to a lesser degree) lacked a theoretical notion of socialism. History since then has indeed taught us many lessons about the essence of socialism as being workers' democracy. The Bolsheviks, however, lacked this understanding; and Farber shows in great detail how this lack led them astray time after time. Carrying the argument about philosophy a step further, if the party is the practical Idea, then, for the Lenin of *State and Revolution*, the soviet is the Notional concretization of the working class as a subject for itself.

Let me try to pull the threads of this article together. What is the dialectic of revolution? First, revolution remains primarily a question of the working class (in a broad sense—those who sell their labor power to live) becoming a revolutionary subject and taking power over the fate of humanity. Second, this involves a dialectic of reform versus revolution within the working class; and this dialectic is subjective, is political, rather than a mechanical question of economic status (such as labor aristocracies). Workers do not all move to a revolutionary position at the same time. Instead, political and philosphic struggle are needed among workers—albeit among workers whose situations differ by workplace, occupation, and time. Revolution thus involves a struggle over politics within the working class as a fundamental aspect of the struggle against the bourgeoisie and the state: first, for the formation of workers' councils and then for the taking of power by these workers' councils. This dialectic is furthered if the revolutionary section of the working class organize themselves as revolutionaries to take direct action (strikes, general strikes, street battles, etc.) before and during the upsurge in class conflict; and to win the great majority of the working class to understand that the seizure of power is needed. Furthermore, since the bourgeoisie has many resources, it is necessary that the winning of the working class and the workers' councils to revolutionary views and action needs to take place quickly.

Where a revolutionary working class party has not been organized (and strong) before the revolutionary situation erupts, the result has been defeat, as in East Germany in 1953, in France in 1968, in Portugal in 1975, and in Poland in the early 1980s. On the other hand, the mere organization of a working class party that is subjectively revolutionary is not a guarantee of victory either over the state or over the possibility of counter-revolution, as is indicated by the failure of the working class, in spite of the strength and revolutionary will of the anarchists, to take and hold power in Spain in the 1930s; and by the failure of Russian workers to keep power due to a combination of objective situations (weakness of Russian economy, of working class as a small minority, and strength of the international bourgeoisie and their militaries) and their subjective lack of understanding of workers' democracy as the key to socialism through the formation of a self-developing working class subject.

What does this mean politically? To me, it suggests that we need to form a revolutionary workers' party. Is this the dreaded "party to lead?" Yes, at certain moments. The organized revolutionary tendency within the working class needs to be able to take initiatives, it needs to be able to speak to the working class as a whole, it needs to be able to help the workers as a whole to organize and win general strikes and the formation of workers' councils, and it needs to be able to win the great majority of other workers to a politics, philosophy, and action for socialist revolution. By any meaning of the terms that I know, this requires that the revolutionary section of the working class needs at least one party, and that this party (or parties) need to act as leaders do. It does NOT mean that the party has to be top-down, or monolithic, or undemocratic. Furthermore, it does not mean that the party (or parties) have to be philosophically united. Indeed, it is my strong suspicion that we need to have parties (or a party) that are open to widespread discussion about the meaning of the dialectic, of what we will do after we take power, etc. if we are going to attract the support of the majority of the working class to revolution (even with the crisis of capitalsim as our best organizer.) It also does not mean that, if we have one party predominant at the moment of the seizure of power by the workers' councils, that this party should necessarily stay dominant after things stabilize (or even until then.) This will be a question of politics and of seeing what is needed. This, too, will be a question of the "sociology of knowledge" in the dialectical sense (and this is where Farber's analysis as well as Anderson's need to be deepened): That revolution is a period of gigantic LEAPS and SLUMPS in people's consciousness; that the process of seizing power teaches lessons of how to organize seizures, and perhaps production and coordination, but also may teach lessons of coercion and terror.

I would suggest, then, that the party that leads the revolution is likely to come out of the process with enormous prestige, with whole sections of the working class nonetheless very annoyed at it, and with a mixture of lessons having been learned by all sections of the working class during the course of revolutionary struggle. Some of these lessons are the basis for the Notion of the working class as the subject to create a new humanity; others are likely to be atrocious and situational in the bad sense (as pertaining to horrible pasts that can now be transcended). This suggests that, at the moment of stabilization of the worldwide revolution (or of major portions thereof), the dialectic of revolution might best be furthered by a process of real splits within the party and then of a reformulation of debates and divisions within the working class—and within the workers' councils—on this basis. I am not enough of a Hegelian philosopher to find the relevant texts, but it might be formulated in terms of the need for, and healthiness of, a negation of the revolutionary working class unity in behalf of the creation of a deeper working class (and human) unity through renewed but primarily peaceful struggle over the emerging new issues of a new era.

In conclusion, then, I am struggling to develop a concept of dialectics and politics that will help us in what we all want: A revolution in which the commodity form is overthrown, workers negate capitalism and their own alienation, and the essential core of the "new subjectivities" can be freed to undergo necessary continuing struggles under conditions where the interests and consciousness of the great majority (the now-in-power working class) are aided by the ending of oppression and the salvation of the planet (rather than having the needs for profitability and a divided working class always creating barriers to these movements' ends). Anderson's book is a useful and brilliant help in our search for this politics, this dialectics, this philosophy. It is not enough, however. Hopefully, these comments will help us move beyond it. I look forward to the brouhaha of friendly debate that might follow the publication of this note.

References
Anderson K. 1995. *Lenin, Hegel, and Western Marxism*. Chicago: University of Illinois Press.
Cole GDH. 1958. *Communism and Social Democracy 1914-1931*. New York: St. Martin's.
Cronin JE. 1980. Labor insurgency and class formation. *Social Science History* 4:125-152.
Dewar H. 1976. *Communist Politics in Britain*. London: Pluto.
Farber S. 1990. *Before Stalinism*. New York: Verso.
Fischer R. 1948. *Stalin and German Communism*. Cambridge: Harvard.
Friedman, SR. 1986. Labor Aristocracy Theories and Worker Politics. *Humanity and Society* 10: 121-145.
Friedman SR. 1983. The theory of the labor aristocracy. *Against the Current* 2 (Fall):24-33.

Hegel. 1989. *Hegel's Science of Logic*. (trans. AV Miller). Atlantic Highlands: Humanities Press International.

Hinton J & Hyman R. 1975. *Trade Unions and Revolution*. London: Pluto.

Kendall W. 1969. *The Revolutionary Movement in Britain 1900-21*. London: Weidenfeld and Nicolson.

Lenin VI. 1972. *Collected Works: v. 38: Philosophical Notebooks*. Moscow: Progress Publishers.

Lorwin VR. 1954. *The French Labor Movement*. Cambridge: Harvard.

Milton N. 1973. *John Maclean*. London: Pluto.

Moore B, Jr. 1978. *Injustice*. White Plains, NY: ME SHarpe.

Nettl P. 1969. *Rosa Luxemburg*. New York: Oxford.

Pelling H. 1958. *The British Communist Party*. London: Adam and Charles Black.

Sirianni C. 1983. Workers' control in Europe. In JE Cronin & C Sirianni (eds.), *Work, Community, and Power*. Philadeplphia: Temple.

Spriano P. 1964. *The Occupation of the Factories*. London: Pluto.

Williams GA. 1973. *Proletarian Order*. London: Pluto.

About the Author

Sam Friedman was born in Richmond, Virginia. He has lived in New Jersey since 1974.

He has published over 140 poems in magazines and journals including *AIDS Care, Canadian Dimension, Haight Ashbury Literary Journal, Lips, Long Shot,* and *Home Planet News.* He is a two-time winner of the *Black Bear Review* Poems of Social Concern competition and won Third Prize in the 2002 National Writers Union Poetry Contest.

He published one chapbook as a benefit for the North American Syringe Exchange Network (*Needles, drugs, and defiance: Poems to organize by,* 1999), and edited a second for them. His third chapbook (*Murders most foul: Poems against war by a World Trade Center survivor,* 2005) was published by the Central Jersey Coalition against Endless War.

In his work as an AIDS researcher, he has published in *Nature, Science, Scientific American, The New England Journal of Medicine, AIDS,* and scores of other journals; and was first author of *Social Networks, Drug Injectors' Lives, and HIV/AIDS.* (Friedman SR, Curtis R, Neaigus A, Jose B, Des Jarlais DC. 1999. New York: Kluwer/Plenum.) He is or has been an Advisory Editor for, or edited special issues for, many journals including *AIDS, JAIDS, AIDS Education and Prevention, AIDS & Public Policy, AIDScience, The Drug and Alcohol Professional, Harm Reduction Journal,* and *Journal of Urban Health.* He currently serves as associate editor for social science for the *International Journal of Drug Policy.*

He is a lifelong social activist and has written many articles on social struggles and socialism. Notable among them are "Making the World Anew in a Period of Workers' Council Rule." *We! Magazine* #63, Volume 2, Number 16 Wednesday, 2 April, 2008. http://www.mytown.ca/we/friedman, and *Teamster Rank and File* (Columbia University Press, 1982.)